THE ASTROT

2019

Horoscope Guide
& Planetary Planner

SCORPIO

CREDITS

Contributing Editor: Suzanne Gerber
Copy Editors: Amy Anthony, Lisa M. Sundry

Cover Art & Zodiac Illustrations by The Grande Dame
www.grandedame.co.uk

Cover Design by Hortasar

ASTROSTYLE

Dedicated to the cherished memory of
Wendell the Love Dachshund (2000-18)

2019

Dear Astro-Friends,

It's been a heck of a ride here on this planet for the last few years, hasn't it? The world has grown more divided than ever—and it's left to the "lightworkers" and changemakers to deal with an existential dilemma. Do we speak up and fight, or are we only yelling into an echo chamber and fanning the flames of conflict? Do we refuse to "feed the dragon" and direct our energies to a higher vibration...or, by doing so, are we being complacent and complicit?

More than ever, we feel hashtag-blessed to have this extra set of divination tools that astrology gives us. Following the stars and planets might not reveal the *entire* story (that's where free will and human choice come in). But an extra layer of insight has helped make sense of some of the madness. Without astrology, we'd feel even more lost at sea!

Our resident numerologist, Felicia Bender, whose annual predictions we proudly include in every edition of this book, wrote in last year's guide about 2018 being a "master number" 11/2 Year. We all felt the paradoxical vibrations of the me-first "1" and the partnership-driven "2" in our lives. Here at Astrostyle, we expanded our staff and collaborated with amazing new people. But it was not without some growing pains.

In Chinese astrology (which we also include in this book), 2019 will be the Year of the Earth Pig. Although Pigs do like to roll around in the mud, they are also highly intelligent and sociable creatures that constantly communicate and cuddle with each other, sleeping nose-to-nose. After the last couple years, we could all use a cosmic group hug!

For 2019, the keyword is "integration." Jupiter, Saturn *and* Neptune will spend the entire year in their "home" signs—the zodiac signs that they rule—which will help stabilize the chaotic energy. And we're moving into a 3 Universal Year according to numerology, which is all about communication and creativity. Hopefully that will spark some productive dialogues and innovative solutions that stick.

The world is far from done with its tumultuous journey—which, we assume, will continue in *some* way for as long as the planet is spinning. But thanks to the stars, we can find some peace with it. For one thing, we're only midway through karmic Neptune's transformational sojourn through its native sign of Pisces (2012-24), a spiritually-awakening transit that happens every 164 years. Chaotic world politics, climate change and other modern crises are pushing the human race to wake up.

But we can't raise our collective vibration to a new frequency unless we get really clear that change starts with *us*. What will that look like in 2019?

Here's our road map for the year, designed to help you direct your energy consciously. How can you use *your* time, attention and resources most effectively? Let's plan it by the planets together.

Ophira & Tali
The AstroTwins

2019 CONTENTS

MOONS, RETROGRADES + ECLIPSES

MAJOR TRENDS: THE OUTER PLANETS

THE 12 SIGNS IN 2019

NUMEROLOGY + CHINESE ASTROLOGY

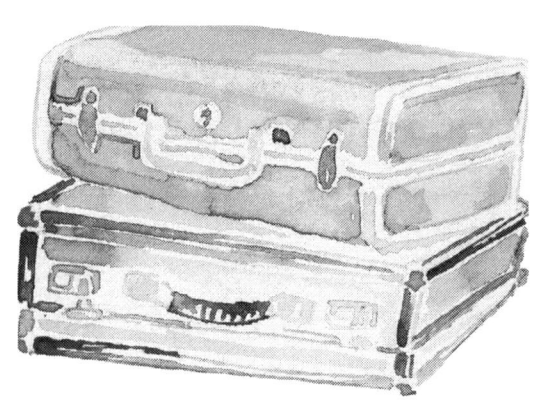

2019 FORECAST
What's in the Stars for All of Us?

Plant your soles on solid ground, but don't take your shoes off and get comfortable just yet. This year's cosmic lineup is an interesting mix of grounding earth-sign energies and motivating fire-sign mojo. After several intense years that have yanked our emotions all over the map, we need to stand firm—if only to regain our centers. But once we reconnect to our truths, it's time to mobilize!

Separation was a hallmark of 2018, which goes on record as one of the most divisive and polarizing years in recent history. With expansive Jupiter spending most of last year in Scorpio, the sign of extremes, it's no surprise. We were pushed to our most intense edges—and it was not easy. With super-sleuth Scorpio in charge, we saw sordid scandals and corruption exposed on a global stage. Things felt deeply karmic and unfair—if not outright confounding. How could this be happening? The rules we've been playing by for so long seemed to be suddenly null and void.

In 2019, hope might once again spring forth. Jupiter will travel through its native turf of Sagittarius until December 2, expanding our viewfinders from tunnel vision into wide-angle settings. With generous Jupiter in this free-spirited sign, we'll be able to see the bigger picture again, and take risks in the name of growth. Global ambassador Jupiter could usher in a more inclusive vibe, with space at the table for everyone. People might actually be nicer to each other, instead of ruthlessly looking out for number one.

We're no traditionalists—nor are we advocates of turning back the clock. But we'll be glad to see some of the timeless values of courtesy, mutual respect and compassion make a comeback this year. In 2019, Jupiter, Saturn, Uranus, Pluto *and* three eclipses will all land in earth signs at various points during the year. Earth energy brings stability and sensuality—it governs the material world. It reminds us to stay present and enjoy what we have.

But in high quantities, earth vibes can also keep us stuck or spinning our wheels. We'll need to make sure we don't get overly set in our ways. Materialism can also run rampant, as the sensory earth signs can get obsessed with accumulating "stuff"—something we don't need at a time when the world's carbon footprint keeps going up way too many shoe sizes.

Luckily, Jupiter won't join this terrestrial tribe until December. Until then, the red-spotted giant will keep the visionary torch burning as he hangs out in fire-sign Sagittarius. Will this leave us with scorched earth… or simply warm us up for the hard work and tenacity that's ahead? Alas, we won't know until we put in the hours and pay our dues.

So…WWJD (What Would Jupiter Do)? In Sagittarius, he'd probably crank up the music, lay out a gourmet spread and turn this hustle into an adventurous party—complete with an open-door policy, a karaoke-friendly soundtrack and plenty of side-splitting jokes.

> **"How can we lighten the density of our spirits? By finding genuine pockets of joy, no matter what's going on around us."**

We'll RSVP "yes" to that, thanks! While many of the world's woes are no laughing matter, self-imposed suffering and seriousness don't ultimately serve anyone. As the stars bring us down to earth in 2019, we've got cosmic permission (make that marching orders) to find magic and mirth in the mundane moments. This year, the best thing we can do (in between fighting for justice, of course) is to relax and enjoy our short time on this earth—with hearts full of gratitude and a leftover case of the giggles.

That's how we can lighten the density of our spirits: by finding genuine pockets of joy, no matter what's going on around us. Only then can we start to transform the fear-based and stagnant energy that's overtaken this planet. By becoming the source of our own happiness, instead of waiting for the world to be "fixed" first, we reclaim our resilience. In fact, this ability might just become a 2019 superpower. Give it a try—the stars are standing at the ready!

Jupiter, Saturn and Neptune in their home signs.

This year, Jupiter will spend 11 months in its home sign of Sagittarius, ruler of global connections and cross-cultural alliances. Jupiter was last here for all of 1983 (the era of huge shoulder pads, Dynasty and Michael Jackson's King of Pop reign, then again in 2006-07, right before the real estate bubble burst. With magnifier Jupiter here, everything will go big and bold.

When a planet is in its "home" sign that means it's visiting the zodiac sign it rules, giving us a double-strength vibration of its energy. This isn't necessarily good or bad—it just means that whatever that force is, we'll experience twice as much of it.

Jupiter's outsized optimism, gregariousness and gambling urges will be matched by its counterpart—stern and structured Saturn, which is also in its home sign of Capricorn. While Jupiter pushes us to "go big or go home," Saturn will ride the brake, demanding that we plan, prepare and think of every worst-case scenario before we go leaping without a parachute.

How about we meditate on it? Spiritual Neptune is also in its home sign of Pisces from 2012 to 2024, continuing to fuel the fanaticism for crystals, astrology, meditation, and ritual that's swept through the world in the past seven years. We can expect more high-vibe hits from Neptune—but hey, we're not complaining. However, this double-strength download from the planet of illusion and self-deception warns against following false prophets and gurus. Looking for answers outside of ourselves, adopting a victim mentality and being utterly unrealistic? Yeah, that's Neptune in Pisces' handiwork, too.

Capricorn dominance: Will patriarchy win...or crumble?

The rooted energy of 2019 comes courtesy of three planets and three eclipses—with a heavy emphasis on Capricorn, the sign of structure, long-term goals and lasting traditions. Capricorn rules institutions, patriarchal society, men, government, big business, fathers and hierarchies. In other words, a lot of the "old school" stuff that people have been working tirelessly to reform and change over the past couple years.

It's been both painful and fascinating to watch. Last year, feminist reporter Hannah Rosin's book *The End of Men* tackles a new vision for the world where gender equality seeps into these outdated systems and institutions. The binary structure of us versus them, winners and losers, male versus female, haves and have nots, now seems hopelessly out of date. With the #MeToo, #TimesUp and #BlackLivesMatter movements accompanying a surge of social activism, feminism, transgender rights, and more—it's clear that we need to make this world

work for more than just a privileged few. Yet, a rise in right-wing nationalism reveals that many people feel threatened by this vision, and will go to extremes to resist a much-needed change.

But in 2019, resistance may be futile. Serious forces of change will be shaking these once solid foundations, even causing some of them to crumble. Structured Saturn and transformational Pluto will both spend all year in Capricorn, making their once-every-35-years conjunction (meetup) in late December. Expansive Jupiter will also move into Capricorn on December 2, pushing us to view old ways through a new lens. And in January, July and December, three eclipses in Capricorn could majorly overturn the way we work, live and conduct business.

Uranus in Taurus: A planet in its "fall."

Adding to the earth-sign cluster, changemaker Uranus will hunker into steady Taurus this March 6, staying until April 2026. This is the side-spinning planet's least favorite sign to visit, because they're such an energetic mismatch. For this reason, Uranus is said to be in "fall" in Taurus.

Uranus made a brief appearance here from May 15 to November 6, 2018, giving us a sneak preview of this tense negotiation. We're being asked to turn the tides without completely capsizing the ship—to make major changes, but not to throw the baby out with the bathwater. It won't be easy, as we'll feel the dueling demands between these cosmic forces.

Chiron in Aries: Healing our self-image.

Reclaim your voice! As wounded healer Chiron, the comet that's now being given near-equal status as the planets, hunkers into individualistic Aries, we're all invited to heal any old pain around feeling invisible, silenced and ill-equipped to manifest our dreams. Naysaying jaws will drop as we scale new personal heights, shedding limiting beliefs and low self-esteem in the process.

Final Leo Eclipse: Leadership renewal?

Will the real leadership please stand up? Oh wait—that person might just be sitting in your chair. This January 21 will bring the final eclipse to ripple across the Leo/Aquarius axis. This series, which started back on February 10, 2017, has been largely responsible for the huge awakening of social justice and activism—as well as for the preening and ego-driven politicians who are pushing party lines instead of representing their constituents. From rallies to protests to demands for policy reform, the eclipses in #woke Aquarius, the sign of groups and humanitarian issues, have revealed the extremes of what can happen when people gather around a common agenda. This final eclipse—a total lunar eclipse and supermoon—will land in regal Leo, giving us one last chance to find our inner sense of dignified authority, and to express it in the world in whatever way, large or small, this feels appropriate.

Numerology: A 3 Universal Year

We're moving out of 2018's intense 11/2 Universal Year in numerology, which pulled us between the contrasts of individualistic "1" energy and the partnership-driven "2." From shifting alliances, selfish agendas and a desperately divided world, navigating that took a lot of inner strength. In 2019, we'll enter a 3 Universal Year, which is all about creativity and communication. Instead of shouting at each other, maybe we'll actually start devising some innovative ways of living that move us past the tired old models.

Chinese Astrology: Year of the Earth Pig

Move over, Rover. After chasing our tails in the Year of the Dog, the Earth Pig waddles in this February 2019. But don't get any "dirty" thoughts: Pigs may play in the mud, but they're some of the smartest and most socially advanced creatures—as well as serious cuddle-monsters! So let's get out of the dog house with its "best in show" competitions and start communing in the keep-it-real open pen. Sounds like hog heaven to us! ✳

NEW & FULL MOONS

Learn to manifest & motivate by the monthly lunar phases.

Following moon cycles is a great way to set goals and reap their benefits. Astrologers believe that our energy awakens at the new moon, then peaks two weeks later at the full moon. In many cultures, farmers have planted by the new moon and harvested by the full moon. Why not get a little lunar boost for your own life?

Every month, the new moon begins a two-week initiating phase that builds up to a full moon, when we reap what we've planted. There is a six-month buildup between new and full moons. Each new moon falls in a specific zodiac sign. Six months later, a full moon occurs in that same zodiac sign.

New moons mark beginnings and are the perfect time to kick off any new projects or idea. Lay the groundwork for what you want to manifest in the coming six months. Set intentions or initiate plans and tend to them for a half year.

Full moons are ideal times for completions, emotional outpourings, and reaping results. They're also your cue to cash in on anything you started at the corresponding new moon six months earlier. What have you been building toward? Full moons act as cosmic spotlights, illuminating what's been hidden. Take stock of your efforts and change course at the full moon. ✳

2019 New Moons

1/5	Capricorn (partial solar eclipse) 8:28pm
2/4	Aquarius 4:03pm
3/6	Pisces 11:03am
4/5	Aries 4:50am
5/4	Taurus 6:45am
6/3	Gemini 6:01am
7/2:	Cancer (total solar eclipse) 3:16pm
7/31	Leo 11:11pm
8/30	Virgo 6:37am
9/28	Libra 2:26pm
10/27	Scorpio 10:05am
11/26	Sagittarius 10:05am
12/26:	Capricorn (solar eclipse) 12:13am

2019 Full Moons

1/21	Leo (total lunar eclipse; supermoon) 12:16 am
2/19	Virgo 10:53am (supermoon)
3/20	Libra 9:42pm (0º) (supermoon)
4/19	Libra 7:12am (29º)
5/18	Scorpio 5:11pm
6/17	Sagittarius 4:30am
7/16:	Capricorn (partial lunar eclipse) 5:38pm
8/15	Aquarius 8:29am
9/14	Pisces 12:32am
10/13	Aries 5:07pm
11/12	Taurus 8:34am
12/12	Gemini 12:12am

Based on Eastern Standard Time (EST)

     The AstroTwins' 2019 Planetary Planner

ECLIPSES

Expect the unexpected: solar and lunar eclipses bring sudden change.

Eclipses happen four to six times a year, bringing sudden changes and turning points to our lives. If you've been stuck in indecision about an issue, an eclipse forces you to act. Unexpected circumstances can arise and demand a radical change of plans.

Truths and secrets explode into the open. Things that aren't "meant to be" are swept away without notice. Shocking as their delivery can be, eclipses help open up space for the new.

The ancients used to hide from eclipses and viewed them as omens or bearers of disruptive change. And who could blame them? They planted, hunted, fished and moved by the cycles of nature and the stars. While the modern astrological approach is not fear-based, we must still respect the eclipses' power.

Solar vs. Lunar Eclipses

There are two types of eclipses—solar and lunar. Lunar eclipses fall at full moons. The earth passes directly between the Sun and the moon, cutting off their communication and casting a shadow on the earth, which often appears in dramatic red and brown shades. A solar eclipse takes place when the new moon passes between the Sun and the earth, shadowing the Sun. The effect is like a spiritual power outage—a solar eclipse either makes you feel wildly off-center, or your mind becomes crystal-clear.

The effects of an eclipse can usually be felt for three to five days before and after the event (some astrologers say eclipses can announce themselves a month before or after, too). Expect the unexpected, and wait for the dust to settle before you act on any eclipse-fueled impulses.

2019 Eclipses

1/5: Capricorn (partial solar eclipse)

1/21: Leo (total lunar eclipse; supermoon)

7/2: Cancer (total solar eclipse)

7/16: Capricorn (partial lunar eclipse)

12/26: Capricorn (annular solar eclipse)

RETROGRADES

When planets go "backward," slowdowns and chaos can ensue.

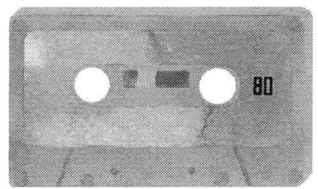

You've heard the hype about retrogrades—but what are they, really? When a planet passes the Earth in its journey around the Sun, it's said to be going retrograde. From our vantage point on Earth, it is almost as if the planet is moving in reverse. This is an illusion, but it's a bit like two trains passing at different speeds—one appears to be going backward. When a planet goes retrograde (for a few weeks, or sometimes even months), everything that falls under its jurisdiction can go a bit haywire.

The most commonly discussed retrograde is Mercury retrograde, which happens 3-4 times a year. Mercury rules communication, travel and technology, and these transits are notorious for crashing computers, causing misunderstandings, delaying flights and even souring deals. Astrologers typically warn against traveling, buying new electronic gadgets or signing legally binding contracts during Mercury retrograde. However, all planets go retrograde at a certain point. Venus reverses course every 18 months; Mars, every two years. The outer planets—Jupiter, Saturn, Uranus, Neptune and Pluto—spend four to five months retrograde every year.

Survival tip: Think of the prefix "re-" when planning the best use of a retrograde. Review, reunite, reconnect, research. Retrogrades aren't the best times to begin something new, but they can be stellar phases for tying up loose ends or giving a stalled mission a second chance. ✳

2019 Retrograde Planets & Dates

MERCURY
March 5–28 (Pisces)
July 7–31 (Leo/Cancer)
October 31–Nov 20 (Scorpio)

JUPITER
April 10–August 11
(Sagittarius)

SATURN
April 29–September 18
(Capricorn)

URANUS
January 1–6 (Aries)
Aug 11, 2019–Jan 11, 2020
(Taurus)

NEPTUNE
June 21–November 27 (Pisces)

PLUTO
April 24–Oct 3 (Capricorn)

CHIRON
July 8–December 12 (Aries)

JUPITER IN SAGITTARIUS

Global connections ignite as Jupiter returns to its home sign from November 8, 2018, until December 2, 2019.

Globalism or bust! Nomadic Jupiter buzzes through its native sign of Sagittarius until December 2, 2019, making #CitizenOfTheWorld the year's most covetable hashtag. There couldn't be a better cosmic cycle for exploring distant corners of the Earth, making friends in far-flung places or visiting your ancestral homeland.

Ready, set, expand! Traveling and connecting cross-culturally.

If life got a little too insular while Jupiter was in private Scorpio from October 10, 2017, to November 8, 2018, then 2019 is the year to make up for lost time. Fire up the Voyager feature on Google Earth and plan a trip to a new city...maybe one that wasn't even on your radar. Set up Duolingo alerts and let the app help you get comfortable with foreign phrases. Engage in philosophical dialogue with people from different cultures and backgrounds. In the year ahead, new innovations such as high-speed planes and trains will shorten the distance between overseas neighbors.

Adventurous types might even live abroad during Jupiter's yearlong phase, or set up a *pied-a-terre* in a second zip code. And no, you don't have to quit your day job to pull that off. While Jupiter cruises through entrepreneurial Sagittarius, the concept of an "office without walls" could become a living reality for many. Companies may choose to hire independent contractors instead of full-time employees. Or, they may adopt a flexible policy, allowing staff to set up remote workstations at home or in a co-working facility.

No matter your GPS coordinates, this is a stellar year to start that kitchen-table side hustle or take your home-based venture into the global market. For those *not* looking to live abroad, global expansion may be as easy as clicking your mouse three times to put in a bid for that job with the Barcelona-based company...or sliding into that across-the-ocean cutie's DMs. Liberation and self-motivation are the name of the game!

Fun fact: The first iPhone was released during Jupiter's last tour of Sagittarius, in June 2007. It's predicted that more than five billion people will have mobile phones by the end of 2019. That's quite the sequel!

Is it time to diversify your romance portfolio? Many people may find themselves making unconventional choices about love or simply opening up to the full array of options before

12

them. Boundless Sagittarians like bicultural beauty Zoe Kravitz and proudly pansexual Janelle Monae will continue to be icons in 2019. Cue Jupiter in Sagittarius' favorite hashtag: #LoveIsLoveIsLOVE.

Border Battles: Immigration and Diversity.

Of course, the "borderless" lifestyle remains, quite sadly, a privileged one in 2019. Native citizenship (read: being lucky enough to be born on the right plot of land) continues to determine who gets to wander freely around the world. The strict and often racially-motivated visa and immigration laws may be a byproduct of repressive Saturn's tour of Sagittarius, which lasted from December 23, 2014, until December 19, 2017. That three-year stronghold intensified much of the xenophobia and strained cultural relations we are dealing with at present. During that cycle, fear of the "other" was bolstered by world events, from refugee crises to border wall frenzies to terrorist bombings in major cities. Politicians around the world capitalized on these emotions and a fierce strain of nationalism emerged. (Interestingly, both "alt-right" nationalist Steve Bannon *and* modernizer Pope Francis are born under the sign of Sagittarius.)

In 2019, Jupiter in Sagittarius will have some cleanup work to do from Saturn's restrictive reign. In many ways, conservative Saturn effectively shut down the

Archer's "we are the world" mindset. Can Jupiter in Sagittarius open up borders again, or will this 13-month cycle shine a high-wattage klieg light on the deep divisions that we humans need to repair?

In the best-case scenario, Jupiter in Sagittarius can be a time of cross-cultural harmony and rekindled diplomacy. When fear is not a barrier, our human instinct is to explore and expand. It was Sagittarius Mark Twain who said, "Travel is fatal to prejudice, bigotry, and narrow-mindedness."

Since Jupiter entered Sagittarius on November 8, 2018, the call to connect cross-culturally has definitely grown louder. If you're lucky enough to live in a diverse city, make a point of expanding your network to include people of different socio-economic backgrounds. Yes, this could take an extra effort, especially with hate crimes statistically rising in major cities since 2014. (You called the cops on her for *what*?!) As Jupiter in Sagittarius reminds us, we all share this planet, and need to learn how to work together.

On the flip side, the double impact of Jupiter in Sagittarius may stoke fanatical fires or increase political extremism and religious fundamentalism. When Jupiter toured Sagittarius in 1924, Ellis Island was closed as an entry port into the U.S. and The Immigration Act was passed, which dramatically limited the number of immigrants allowed into the country.

Jupiter in Sagittarius will force us to deal with the lingering divisiveness. The battle lines might be drawn based on culture—or they may dissolve completely as people unify across socio-economic barriers to create a working solution for all. We could see major political leaders rise and fall. During past Jupiter in Sagittarius transits, Gandhi and Yitzhak Rabin were murdered, the Dalai Lama fled Tibet while Margaret Thatcher and Fidel Castro took power. The Nixon Watergate scandal also played out while Jupiter was in Sagittarius during the early 1970s.

Jupiter and Sagittarius are also associated with the creation of law—after all, Jupiter, a.k.a. Zeus, was the god of all gods in Greek mythology. International trade agreements may be rewritten before the end of 2019, while we may see more revolutions in unstable nations, especially where the resources are kept in the hands of the privileged few. Sagittarius is a fire sign, and rising heat levels may be a driving force behind uprisings, as populations are forced to move around for survival needs like food and water. During Jupiter's last visit to Sagittarius, in 2007, a major drought in Australia caused wheat crop production to fail and prices to increase around the world. Of course, necessity has always been the mother of invention, and new industries may emerge as others dwindle.

Educate and Edu-tain.

High-minded Sagittarius also rules media, education, and philosophical thought. With self-publishing tools creating a golden age for authors, 2019 will be a renaissance for media makers, teachers and students. Want to lead your own workshop or develop an online course? Or maybe it's time to circulate that dystopian sci-fi novel that's been sitting, fully edited, on your hard drive. Try out tools like Udemy or Amazon Createspace and spread the knowledge.

College retention may also come into the spotlight while Jupiter is enrolled in Sagittarius University for most of 2019. With student debt reaching record levels in the U.S., the ivory tower is less of a "next logical step" for the country's high school graduates. The call for affordable education could become louder. Online accreditations and even charter universities may grow in enrollment as adventurous Jupiter pushes the envelope.

Not the bookish type? No problem. Since jovial Jupiter loves to *edu-tain* (educate + entertain), opt for experiential learning. Enroll in a yoga retreat—or circus school! Train for a marathon. Or gain a new skill with an immersion program. How about spending eight months literally getting your hands dirty at The Organic Farm School? Or take the ultimate challenge during this outspoken cycle and try a ten-day Vipassana silent meditation.

This quiet timeout can connect you with your most profound thoughts, and *after* that, you can fully unleash! Turn those ideas into a full-length album or diversity-training workshop...or some sort of teachable moment!

Speaking of global education, studies show that educating girls and women is the key to eradicating worldwide poverty. If you're looking for a worthwhile cause to get behind in 2019, may we suggest educational reform for girls? One in three girls is married before age 18 in developing nations, and pregnancy complications are the leading cause of death for girls age 15 to 19 worldwide. By contrast, when girls are educated, they can contribute to their economies, breaking the cycle of hunger and poverty. As self-sufficient citizens, they are less likely to contract diseases that ravage their communities and cause widespread deaths.

Ambassador Jupiter in Sagittarius could inspire art, music, comedy and eye-opening memes that give us a window into other worlds. While Jupiter was last here at the start of the 1970s, (Aries) Clive Campbell, aka Kool DJ Herc, put the poverty-stricken South Bronx on the map. Using two turntables to isolate the "breakbeat," he fathered modern-day hip-hop—a genre that, to this day, remains both a celebration of black culture and an oft-political megaphone for the African diaspora.

History repeats itself.

Jupiter only visits each sign every 12-13 years. The red-spotted planet's last tour of Sagittarius was from November 24, 2006, until December 18, 2007. Flip back in your calendar and have a look. What were you doing during that period last decade? You may see themes from that time in your life emerge once again. This is a time for letting adventure lead the way; for taking more risks in the name of expansion.

For Tali, 2007 marked her inaugural pilgrimage to Burning Man, an annual event in the Nevada desert that has "Jupiter in Sagittarius" written all over. Think: camping, utopian ideals, experimental communities living together, heady philosophical moments punctuated by childlike wonder and joy, and of course...fire! Burning Man turned out to be more than a lark. When Tali returned to Black Rock City, NV in 2008, she met her husband Cory in their shared camp, then moved from New York to Seattle and married at Burning Man in 2009. They've been going annually ever since; a meaningful and adventurous honeymoon sojourn, and a chance to collaborate creatively and innovatively as a pair.

So, get ready! The "wild gambles" that Jupiter in Sagittarius may churn up could manifest more than you bargained for. (Like, say, a spouse and a cross-country move.) With stakes *that* high, however, do look before you leap. The point is to jump into an exciting new realm—and land on your feet! ✳

The AstroTwins' 2019 Planetary Planner

JUPITER IN CAPRICORN

Calculated risks and growth within a structured plan? We'll navigate this paradox as daring Jupiter visits cautious Capricorn from December 2, 2019, until December 19, 2020.

Ask, believe...achieve! On December 2, 2019, jovial Jupiter soars to the top of the zodiac wheel, joining stalwart Saturn and power-obsessed Pluto in Capricorn until December 19, 2020. Clarify goals and map out those milestones! The groundswell of ambition that's been percolating since Jupiter's counterpart, Saturn, entered Capricorn in late 2017 could reach a fever pitch during this 12-month cycle. With Jupiter's foot on the accelerator, stalled missions will forge ahead. Competition could get fierce as we all find ourselves on a quest to become our best. And we're sure to see some unprecedented developments in government, economy and corporate policies—all realms over which Capricorn presides.

There *is* a catch here, though. Jupiter is in "fall" in Capricorn, its most challenging position on the zodiac wheel. Many of the red-spotted planet's free-flowing and inclusive traits are muffled in the sign of the Sea Goat. By nature, Jupiter wants to swing out and take a risk, while Capricorn can be sober and discerning. Jupiter says, "All are welcome!" while Capricorn wants to curate an elite crew. There will be moments throughout this yearlong cycle where we feel as if we are pumping the gas and riding the brake at the same time! Our

gambling instincts could miss the mark—or even lead to corrupt choices if we leap before we look. Conversely, we may become *so* risk averse that we get stuck in archaic traditions that stall progress.

Capricorn's perfectionistic tendencies can be amplified by Jupiter's beams. Even if you are sitting on a million-dollar idea, you may be hesitant to move forward after December 2. One of the key lessons of Jupiter in Capricorn? Learning how to fail faster and bounce back quicker. After all, "mistakes" are part of the process. At the same time, don't overdo it on the trial and error—not only will that be expensive, but you might waste precious time reinventing a pre-existing wheel.

Jupiter in masterful Capricorn is a prime time to work with pro-level mentors and experts who can help you map out sound strategies for long-term growth. Capricorn is the zodiac's structure junkie and architect; it doesn't create legends, it creates legacies, baby!

A green business boom.

Expansion and growth are the holy grails of the modern age. Normally, "can't stop, won't stop" Jupiter feels right at home in this wildly excessive mindset. But under earth-guardian Capricorn's

16

watch, progress must be harnessed and directed. More isn't necessarily *more* during this transit. Jupiter in clean, green Capricorn wants us to evaluate our footprints and then assess the impact that our empires have on the environment.

With natural resources dwindling and our water systems becoming alarmingly polluted, Jupiter in earth-sign Capricorn is a clarion call for sustainable businesses. Clean energy, like solar and wind, could grow in popularity as residential solutions. Developments in hybrid and electric vehicles could take an unprecedented leap. Companies like Starbucks have already begun to ban plastic straws and many major cities like Seattle now charge for grocery bags and have implemented a paper-only policy.

Mega-retailer H&M has already enacted a textile recycling program, inviting customers to drop off their unwanted garments to be repurposed into everything from insulation to carpet padding. We expect more corporations to shift in this direction— if only in the interest of capturing the younger, environmentally aware market.

Ballers or bailers?

In financially savvy Capricorn, Jupiter can act as an abundance agent—or a giant magnifier of our economic state of affairs. Whatever Jupiter

touches, it expands. If you've been manifesting consciously, it may soon feel like someone poured Miracle-Gro on your balance sheet. Hello, baller! This is a golden era for business-savvy types. Is it time to step into being the CEO of your own company or to step into greater leadership at your day job? Jupiter in Capricorn will spur you on.

On the downside, the galactic gambler's tour of success-obsessed Capricorn can make some folks susceptible to get-rich-quick schemes. People who have taken shortcuts to the top could also be exposed—and forced to move way back on the game board. Jupiter in Capricorn may reveal corrupt corporate practices, forcing us to "vote with our dollars" by aligning with ethical companies. Executives may be forced to step down over scandals (most likely in the form of mismanagement of finances or HR violations), carving out a space for rising stars to settle on those thrones.

Jupiter's last visit to Capricorn—from December 18, 2007, to January 5, 2009—serves as a cautionary tale of what *not* to do in 2019-20. This marked a major moment for the global economy, and not in a good way. Like a stadium klieg light, Jupiter exposed the fault lines in the failed banking system as the Federal Reserve and U.S. government were forced to bail out financial institutions. The stock

         The AstroTwins' 2019 Planetary Planner

market crashed and Wall Street goliaths, including Goldman Sachs and Bear Stearns, fell to their knees. Taxpayers had to bail out U.S. mortgage companies Fannie Mae and Freddie Mac. The real estate market took a major hit; homes plunged in value and record numbers foreclosed—while others discovered, in late 2008, that their life savings had been stolen by Bernie Madoff's firm. The toll was *major*!

In 2008, while Jupiter was in Capricorn, the United States elected the first ever African American as President. One of Barack Obama's first tasks? To put an "economic stimulus plan" in place to repair the shattered financial state of the nation.

Will we be on the right side of history this time around? It's almost anyone's guess as alliances shift and trade wars erupt. Stabilizing the world economy may become mission critical in 2020—which might mean embracing Jupiter's globalist mindset and working closely with other nations to fortify the collective good.

A new men's movement?

Capricorn is the sign associated with the masculine gender. As high-minded Jupiter tours the cosmic boys' club, men will be called forth to "educate and elevate" themselves. While a handful of men, including the late Anthony Bourdain, were outspoken advocates for the #MeToo movement, many dudes have remained quiet, supporting the movement from the background. The idea that women's rights are human rights—not "simply" a feminist agenda—may gather steam while Jupiter is in Capricorn. Men speaking up and speaking out

for equality could become a widespread trend in late 2019. Our fingers are certainly crossed.

Simultaneously, the so-called patriarchy (also Capricorn's domain) could gather its own momentum. We may see more backlash from an entitled group of men who are afraid that sharing the power means losing "their" power. With controlling Pluto in Capricorn from 2008 to 2024 and rigid Saturn here from December 2017 until December 2019, fears have been provoked, causing people to cleave to conservative values.

As Jupiter enters the picture, that collective resistance to change might loosen up. We don't have to throw out the baby with the bathwater, but could we update some of those traditions, taking the best and leaving the rest? Since Jupiter is also the lawmaker, the new structures we invent between December 2, 2019, and December 19, 2020, could be taken to the high courts for legislation. Here's hoping dynamics truly evolve throughout all of our societal structures—instead of merely dissolving into a giant, cosmic arm-wrestling match. ✷

SATURN IN CAPRICORN

Structured Saturn roots into its home sign of Capricorn from December 19, 2017, until December 17, 2020. With potent Pluto also here, deep structural changes are ahead.

How stable is your base? In 2019, astro-architect Saturn will spend the second of three years in its home sign of Capricorn, inspecting for "structural flaws." Are you building your dreams in the most sensible way? Did you apply for the proper permits and pass the tests with flying colors? If not, oops! You may have to contend with penalties and aggravating do-overs before those blueprints can be sent to production.

Saturn returns to Capricorn every 28 to 30 years, staying for about three years each time. Its imprint on history is indelible, tearing down outmoded structures and revealing some of the worst corruptions among world leadership. Saturn was last in Capricorn from February 13 to June 9, 1988, and then November 11, 1988, to February 6, 1991. If you can remember back that far, you may see recurring themes.

Can the weak spots be fixed with a remodel or retrofit...or is this job a total teardown? Steel your resolve: If something needs to be repaired, a simple patch-up won't do in 2019.

There *is* a silver lining to this overwhelming rebuild. Since Saturn's in its element in Capricorn, we'll be primed to tackle outsized challenges, even if we have no clue where the ultimate solution lies. While 2018 exposed the metaphoric cracks in our systems, in 2019, we can begin the restructuring work. As harsh as Saturn's audits can be, they are ultimately supportive. The goal is to help us strengthen our foundations, so we can keep "up-zoning" our plans and providing sustenance for generations to come. Where will this hit the hardest? Both Saturn and Capricorn rule the following areas: authorities (such as heads of states and CEOs), corporations, governments, the economy, father figures and the "masculine" realm.

Body-wise, our bones and teeth are associated with this planet and zodiac sign—and it's fitting. The skeletal system literally holds up our bodies like the steel beams of a high-rise skyscraper. The bones and teeth take the longest to decompose, a metaphor for the legacy that both Saturn and Capricorn inspire us to leave behind. On that note, pump up your calcium intake in 2019, and incorporate more nondairy (and thus, easier on the planet) sources such as seeds (chia and poppy), dark leafy greens (kale, spinach and collard greens), beans and lentils.

The patriarchy also falls under Saturn in Capricorn's domain, which has been both maligned and strengthened in 2018. Part of the reason for that is because volcanic, domineering Pluto is also in Capricorn from 2008 to 2024, riding tandem through Capricorn during Saturn's entire voyage through this zodiac sign. Talk about a double whammy of intensity! With the confirmation of Brett Kavanaugh to the Supreme Court last fall, the majority-male GOP gained the most power over the U.S. government since the Great Depression.

In 2019, we may see more shenanigans from the "good old boys" and entitled "bro culture." And since Saturn also rules limits and restrictions, this is bound to create pushback from the gender equality movement. Women's rights groups will continue to mobilize, a la Linda Sarsour's historical Women's March and the #TimesUp effort which was ignited on January 1, 2018, just weeks after Saturn shifted into Capricorn. Employees will demand stronger protection policies—as hundreds of McDonalds workers did in October 2018, when they staged a strike to protest sexual harassment.

Men who embody the "divine masculine" may emerge as allies to women, raising the bar for male behavior in 2019. The battle is bound to be discouraging at times, given Saturn's slow evolution towards results. Willpower is a must!

By the same token, this cycle may continue to reveal the most egregious acts of sexism within corporations and governments. The polarizing revelations will continue to take down some men abusing their power while handing others a pass because of their privileged stations in society.

In earth sign Capricorn, Saturn's magnifying glass will scan for flaws in the foundation of leadership and large entities, including their environmental impact. As global temperatures and sea levels rise, we will be forced to deal with the deleterious impact that consumer culture has on the planet. While stubborn Saturn makes us struggle to change our "standard operating procedures," corporations may have no choice but to do things differently.

In 2019, savvy retailers should rethink the long-held strategy of "overstock the shelves." Given the massive amounts of textiles and uneaten grocery products sent to landfills each year, innovation seems imminent. Will VR kiosks to "try on" clothes replace the overstuffed racks? Could wider aisles, cooking demonstrations—and even food banks—become the new grocery store norm?

It's time for some reimagining, especially as customers become more eco-savvy and concerned with the fate of this third rock from the Sun. Customization and "on-demand" production may become *au courant*, even if that means waiting longer for the drones to drop packages on our doorsteps.

Saturn & Pluto in Capricorn: An Unsettling Match.

With transformational Pluto also in Capricorn from 2008 to 2024, there are seismic shifts going on beneath the surface, sort of like tectonic plates move before an earthquake. Powerful, controlling Pluto deals in secrets and hidden motives. This shadowy planet can expose corruption, or it can alchemize it, raising us to a higher spiritual vibration. Saturn demands integrity and creates breakdowns that force us to do the repair work. In many ways, these planetary players are opposites: Pluto rules the esoteric realm, while Saturn governs all that is tangible and concrete. This can also be like a metaphorical volcano rumbling beneath our feet, pushing us to face facts before a situation explodes.

Will Saturn shape Pluto's changes into reality or will their joint effort cause more destruction and greed? Saturn and Pluto travel in the same sign every 33 to 38 years. Historically, their union has recalibrated the global power dynamics. They were conjunct in October 1914, near the outbreak of World War I. In 1948, their close alliance in Leo coincided with Israel's formation and a redistribution of power in the Middle East. The 1982 Saturn-Pluto meetup, in balanced Libra, was a time of economic recession with the highest unemployment rate since the Great Depression (which, incidentally, took place during Saturn's 1929-32 visit to Capricorn).

As Saturn and Pluto make their way through Capricorn, we'll feel their joint impact in government, business and the economy. People will transform the way they work, conduct commerce and deal with hierarchies, perhaps forming their own micro-economies or self-regulating communities.

We're hoping the end result will be greater clarity and leaders who are truly "for the people." But we may not know fully until January 12, 2020, when these planetary players make an exact meetup (conjunction). From December 20, 2019 until February 5, 2020, they'll be in ultra-close connection, so expect to feel it then. We've already experienced the tremors leading up to this. In 2018, befuddling summits shifted global alliances. Meetings between the U.S. and long-sworn "enemies of state" such as Russia and North Korea created polarizing spectacles—and non-spectacles since, in true Plutonian fashion, most of the "negotiating" took place in total secrecy. Meanwhile, trade agreements came under fire between long-time allies and peaceful global alliances turned into jaw-dropping power struggles.

The upheaval has left some people feeling safer and others totally ungrounded. In 2019, Year Two of Saturn's tour of Capricorn, we may see the theatrics level off a bit as the taskmaster planet clamps down on Pluto's sneak attacks.

Saturn in Capricorn through history: Surprising twists.

To understand what Saturn in Capricorn could bring, it's helpful to review past eras for recurring themes. Saturn's prior visits to Capricorn have brought major "people versus the government" movements. Dictators have risen to power while others came crashing down. Saturn is the great cosmic teacher, and at its best, it can reveal

         The AstroTwins' 2019 Planetary Planner

impressive leaders who rule with integrity, making historic diplomatic moves.

Powerful leaders protecting the people & environment.

Saturn was in Capricorn in the early 1900s, when U.S. President Teddy Roosevelt, famous for anti-trust laws and "trust-busting," took office. Roosevelt, whose face is carved into Mount Rushmore, was known as "the conservationist president" for his pioneering efforts to protect wildlife and public parks. After creating the United States Forest Service, he established 150 national forests and protected about 230 million acres of public land.

Since Saturn moved into earth-sign Capricorn on December 19, 2017, the U.S. has seen its largest rollback in protections of federal lands in the country's history. The U.S. Interior Secretary is working to legalize offshore drilling on the coastlines which have been battered by shifting weather patterns and rising sea levels. Here's hoping Roosevelt's legacy rises again—our planet literally depends on it.

Activism & Women's Suffrage.

Roosevelt was also a driving force behind the Progressive Movement of the early 20th century, which organized to combat problems created by industrialization, urbanization and government corruption. It was a Saturn in Capricorn crackdown on the waste, greed and excess of the Gilded Age. Corporate trusts, in cahoots with corrupt politicians, were targeted by the Progressive Movement, which pushed for fair wages and the eight-hour workday.

Prohibition, which outlawed alcohol, also rose during this conservative Saturn in Capricorn era.

Women's suffrage thrived during this period, as activists gathered and fought for the right to vote. It was a well-timed challenge to the patriarchy, as women demanded to be let into male-only institutions they'd been excluded from. The feminist ideal of the New Woman—a bicycle-riding, educated, independent figure—skyrocketed as Saturn entered Capricorn in the 20th century. In 2018-19, the hashtag heroines are bringing women together, such as Tarana Burke whose #MeToo movement was re-energized by Alyssa Milano just before Saturn entered Capricorn.

The Great Depression.

Saturn entered Capricorn in March 1929, briefly backing into Sagittarius from May until November of that year. That summer, the stock market peaked and began declining, due in part to the faltering agricultural economy, excessive bank loans and a proliferation of debt. On October 29, 1929, also known as Black Thursday, the stock market crashed. While Saturn returned to Capricorn from November 29, 1929, until February 1932, the Great Depression devastated the U.S. economy. By the time Saturn left this sign, stocks were only worth 20 percent of their 1929 value, nearly half of America's banks had failed and 30 percent of the workforce was unemployed.

While we are not predicting a market crash simply because Saturn is returning to Capricorn, there is an undeniable bubble, brought on in part by the euphoric early stage of tax cuts and breaks. But as the U.S. federal deficit rises as a result, the Federal

Reserve may be forced to elevate interest rates to keep inflation under control. Some financial analysts are predicting a forthcoming crash as early as 2019. While we wouldn't be so bold as to say this *will* happen, if Wall Street has shown us anything, it's that history repeats itself. Pro tip: If you're purchasing or refinancing property or taking out a loan, lock in lower, fixed interest rates fast!

Fidel Castro & the Cold War.

Saturn entered Capricorn once again on January 5, 1959. Four days prior, Fidel Castro ousted the Capricorn dictator Fulgencio Batista. Soon after, Russia and Cuba got cozy and the Cold War began, leading to a slew of embargos that were lifted by Barack Obama, then reimposed by Donald Trump. As Saturn was leaving Capricorn in 1961, John F. Kennedy, Jr. came to power and the Bay of Pigs invasion attempted and failed to remove Castro, who went on to become one of the longest ruling heads of state in history.

Gandhi's Passive Resistance movement.

While Saturn toured Capricorn in 1930, Mohandas Gandhi led the Salt March—one of the most famous examples of passive resistance *(satyagraha)*. For 50 years, salt manufacturing was controlled by a government monopoly. Although salt was easily procured from the sea, it was a crime for Indian citizens to make or get their own salt, because the government charged a tax on it. Gandhi encouraged citizens to refuse this tax by making their own salt or buying it from underground sellers. The 24-day, 240-mile Salt March ended at a beach when Gandhi picked up a handful of salt and held it overhead as a symbol of peaceful protest. This passive resistance movement ultimately led to India's independence from British rule 17 years later. Can justice be obtained through peaceful activism in 2019? It's hard to say. But more than ever, we're seeing proof of Gandhi's words that, "An eye for an eye only ends up making the whole world blind."

Stalin's Collectivization: Socialism gone wrong.

In the Soviet Union, an inhumane attempt at government intervention during Saturn's transit through Capricorn led to one of history's worst atrocities. In the early 1930s, Joseph Stalin forced rural farmers to "collectivize" their land, agriculture and livestock, turning over all output to government control. This was touted as a modern miracle: The means of production would be "socialized" and removed from individual control, allowing (ostensibly) for more equal distribution of food. Many farmers protested through acts of sabotage: refusing to produce and harvest crops or even burning theirs. The more successful and rebellious farmers were shot, deported or put in horrific Gulag labor camps. Collectivism created such huge upheaval around food production that it led to the Soviet famine of 1932-33, which had a death toll of 5 to 10 million Ukrainians. Worse, Stalin withheld huge reserves of grain from the citizens that could have relieved the famine.

Since Saturn re-entered Capricorn, the tariffs and counter-tariffs imposed between the U.S. and Mexico, Canada, the E.U. and China have hit some farmers hard. Hardline immigration policies

   The AstroTwins' 2019 Planetary Planner

have also impacted many agricultural and livestock businesses who rely on migrant workers for labor.

Build bridges, not walls: Construction & deconstruction.

Saturn and Capricorn rule constructions and boundaries—including literal walls. The Berlin Wall was built during Saturn's visit to Capricorn in 1961 as a way of stopping Eastern Bloc emigration into Western Europe. This links back to the previous time Saturn was in Capricorn, as people were fleeing Soviet-style regimes created under Stalin's rule. History came full circle when Saturn returned to Capricorn from 1988-91. The Berlin Wall was opened in 1989, and its demolition was underway for the rest of this Saturn transit. As Saturn moves into Capricorn again, Donald Trump continues to press for a U.S.-Mexico border wall.

On a positive note, an architectural renaissance could be in order. Saturn in Capricorn can help us leave impressive (and positive) legacies that stand the test of time. Saturn rules buildings and architecture, and we may see some great new innovations in this arena, especially in the green and sustainable building genre. (Think: solar energy and living roofs for food production in urban areas.) While Saturn was in Capricorn from 1959-61, Frank Lloyd Wright finished the spectacular Guggenheim Museum, his last masterpiece before his death.

Saturn in Capricorn: Lessons moving forward.

How can we prevent troubling history from repeating itself as Saturn returns to Capricorn, placing a double dose of emphasis on systems, governments and authority? We must watch out for oppressive laws and ideologies masquerading as "revolutions." From North Korea's Kim Jong Un (a Capricorn) to Syria's Bashar Al Assad to Venezuela's Nicolas Maduro to Russia's Vladimir Putin, we are trekking through this Saturn in Capricorn cycle with perilous international leadership—and scary examples of patriarchal, authoritarian domination gone awry.

Since Saturn suppresses and Pluto transforms, this era might eventually put the kibosh on heavy-handed rulership and patriarchy. As Saturn clamps down on Capricorn's masculine rulership, we may see a rise in female government leaders and women business owners. Statistics show that educating girls and women is one of the vital keys to ending poverty. As women's participation in the workforce grows and conscious men help usher in the "divine masculine," gender roles will continue to be reformed. Here's hoping that men and women can work together in service of the planet's survival, uniting around the common cause of our shared humanity. ✳

The AstroTwins' 2019 Planetary Planner   24

URANUS IN TAURUS

The economy and tradition get an overhaul as Uranus enters Taurus from March 6, 2019, until April 26, 2026.

Snap your final duck-lipped selfies and binge-watch *Game of Thrones* (again). Until March 6, Uranus—the planet that rules technology and community—runs one last lap through Aries, the zodiac's "me first" warrior, before taking up residence in traditional Taurus again on March 6. Uranus only visits each zodiac sign every 84 years, electrifying the airwaves for about seven years and disrupting the status quo.

However, Uranus is in its "fall" in Taurus—a weakened position—since the energies are an awkward mismatch. Unconventional Uranus pushes for radical evolution and progress, while nostalgic Taurus roots into time-tested traditions, resisting change at every turn. Talk about an odd couple mashup!

We got our first taste of this seismic cultural shift last year. On May 15, 2018, the side-spinning planet poked its head into the Bull's pen, igniting a bizarre blend of avant-garde and old-fashioned energies. But due to its annual retrograde, Uranus backed into Aries on November 6, 2018, giving us one last round of the Ram's nearly eight-year tour of duty.

Uranus in Aries: Where we're coming from.

When combative, combustible Uranus first joined Aries' "fight club" on March 11, 2011, a magnitude 9.1 tsunami devastated much of Tokyo and caused an emergency in the nearby Fukushima nuclear plant. Shortly thereafter, storms erupted on the political front, beginning with the Arab Spring, then Occupy Wall Street in September of 2011. Throughout this entire Uranus cycle, marginalized groups have raised their voices in the name of inclusion and human rights. Uranus in Aries brought us the Black Lives Matter movement, the Marriage Equality Act, the Women's March, Transgender Awareness Week, and #TimesUp.

On the hotheaded flipside, Uranus in Aries also stirred a few frightening fringe uprisings, including ISIS and violent "alt-right" rallies. Autocratic rulers were emboldened, such as Russia's Vladmir Putin and his army of hackers, and Nicolas Maduro whose reign has caused a total economic collapse in Venezuela. Televised missiles were on military parade in North Korea. In the U.S., mass shootings (many in schools) have caused unthinkable grief, intensifying clashes between gun-rights activists and citizens like the students of Florida's Marjory Stoneman Douglas High School. And just as this cycle began with "fire and fury," it leaves acres of burned forests and islands devastated by hurricanes in its wake.

Television, which falls under Uranus' domain, has gone through a revolution since 2011. Behemoth networks lost market shares to indie productions from Amazon and Netflix, bringing us explosively popular shows like *Stranger Things* and *Orange Is the New Black*. YouTube stars are the new self-made celebrities, raking in major sponsorships and earnings that are not dependent on a Hollywood agent. The legacy of Uranus in Aries? Your shot at fame might just require a smartphone and a smile.

In many ways Uranus in Aries woke up the fighters in all of us. Activists found their voices, social justice warriors rallied for dramatic protests from airports to campuses to major cities. In true Aries fashion, there was even a tinge of "street theater" to some of these gatherings with flash mobs and props like pussy hats. In some cases, it felt more like a Roman Colosseum, complete with raw aggression, loud group chanting and torches.

While these outlets for collective rage have swung between jaw-dropping and cathartic, the question remains: Where is it all leading us? And what is it *really* going to take to create lasting change?

Uranus in Taurus: Where we're going now.

With Uranus in "brass tacks" Taurus, the revolution may be quieter, counting its wins in a newly quantifiable way. As the first of the earth signs, the Bull pulls our attention down to the level of the roots from which everything stems. To solve a crisis between 2019 and 2026, we will have to drill to the very base level (and preferably not with a fracking device).

The Bull's motto is "lather, rinse, repeat." Between March 6, 2019, and April 26, 2026, a consistent effort will be required to ignite Uranus' revolutionary powers. We're betting that stamina will be tested, especially in this era of short attention spans. Instead of popping up for a weekend protest when something pisses us off, we will have to roll up our sleeves and get to work on the less "glamorous" stuff like reforming policies, attending city council meetings (over and over again), and organizing grassroots efforts.

When Uranus was in Taurus from 1850-59, Harriet Tubman became a major conductor of the Underground Railroad, risking her life through her quiet heroics as she helped to lead enslaved Africans to safety. In the spirit of rooted Taurus,

> **"Uranus in sensible, profit-driven Taurus helps us monetize our creations in new ways."**

it was literally an underground job, the quietest revolution that had an immensely profound impact.

Follow the money.

In recent years, the chasm between the "haves" and the "have-nots" has widened, as the middle class shrinks. Despite glowing economic reports of low unemployment rates and tax cuts, it remains to be seen if Wall Street will remain a bull market— even as Uranus cries, "Toro!" Interestingly, the Boston Tea Party took place during a previous Uranus in Taurus cycle, when demonstrators protested "taxation without representation." And the U.S. spent the entire last Uranus in Taurus transit climbing out of the Great Depression, which ended in 1941, right as Uranus departed from Taurus. President Roosevelt also signed the U.S. Social Security act, providing unemployment compensation and pensions for the elderly.

In Taurus, Uranus urges us to "follow the money" to discover who is *really* pulling the purse strings. Campaign finance reform may become a hot-button issue as citizens examine the way economic power has altered the political landscape—so much so that most modern-day government officials rely on outside funding to afford the high-dollar TV spots and other "publicity" required to keep pace with their contenders. As a result, their major donors may have as much of a sway as the constituents they represent. Will politicians reveal their funding sources or fight harder to keep their alliances under wraps? It remains to be seen.

Dollars go digital.

With technological Uranus in money-minded Taurus, mobile payment apps like Venmo and Apple Pay may continue to replace printed money. Self-checkouts are taking the place of live cashiers in many major retailers and cryptocurrency is still, well, cryptic to many and lucrative to others. Sensible Taurus could change the type of businesses that get funded. Rather than sink a load of venture capital into yet another social-sharing app, startup support may go to practical inventions that improve our daily lives. Of course, as A.I. replaces human labor, our relationship with money could go through a massive shift. Out of necessity, people may adopt the barter system, or take up the "gift economy" that's practiced at festivals like Burning Man. In this model, no cash changes hands, and goods or services are offered from a spirit of generosity.

The gig economy will continue to rise with indie-spirited Uranus in hardworking Taurus. More people will work remotely and in co-working spaces, and the full-time employment model may continue to wane. The Uranus in Aries cycle brought us opportunities to unshackle ourselves from the nine-to-five lifestyle, with solo venture options such as Airbnb, Lyft, and co-op offices like WeWork (and the all-women's space The Wing, one of our favorites!) gaining massive popularity. But there are also drawbacks, such as a lack of benefits and no actual ownership of assets. For the coming seven years, people may trend more toward owning a "share" of these places, perhaps receiving stock options in a company where they are independent contractors, or building equity instead of just getting a check.

> **"We may see scientific developments that revolutionize the farming industry."**

world may be totally transformed between now and 2026. An example of this is the world's food industry. The documentary *Wasted* pulls back the curtain, reporting that 40 percent of the world's edible production goes to waste—and 90 percent of the discarded food in the U.S. winds up in landfills. Meanwhile, approximately 800 million people on the planet are starving.

Uranus in sensible, profit-driven Taurus can help us monetize our creations in interesting new ways. Taurus rules the physical world and material objects. With freedom-seeking Uranus in sensual Taurus, we'll want to enjoy our possessions without being chained to them. While you'll be wise to downsize and accumulate less, financially-prudent Taurus still urges us to invest wisely for the long haul. Time to become savvier about saving, and discerning with our *dinero*.

Changes to farming and the food supply.

While Taurus is a creature of comfort, Uranus in this sign will challenge us to enjoy luxury without sacrificing sustainability. The very systems that have made modern life so convenient for the Western

With forward-thinking Uranus here, we may see scientific developments that improve soil quality, help growers and revolutionize the farming industry. Can we pioneer a solution to global hunger—one that doesn't involve factory farms and genetically modified seeds?

At this writing, scientists are developing 3D and 4D "printed" food that's actually edible. The saying "let food be thy medicine and medicine be thy food" doesn't only apply to your $15 chia seed pudding with young coconut meat. In 2017, scientists successfully transformed a spinach leaf into a working human heart muscle. With Uranus in Taurus, we may look to the earth beneath our feet, rather than the latest chemical concoction, to fight diseases.

The rise of populism and dictatorship.

The worst manifestations of Uranus in Taurus can be bigotry, stubbornness and warmongering. Adolf Hitler, a Taurus, seized power just as Uranus was ending its last transit of Aries, and retained his dictatorial grip through the 1930s, while Uranus was in Taurus. Mussolini also came into power during this last Uranus in Taurus transit, spreading fascism. As we enter the same cycle 84 years later, extreme right-wing candidates are once again on the rise, spinning propaganda through social media, slanted news outlets, populist rallies and cyber hacking. In the past few years, Uranus in Aries has provoked violent disruptors, many using technology to plot public acts of terrorism or to spread messages of hate. Hopefully, we will learn from history and not underestimate the "fringe" groups' ability to organize and gain critical mass.

From virtual reality to mixed reality.

Uranus in sensory Taurus will alter the way we interact with the physical and digital worlds. The VR world is developing ways to include smell, touch and taste from afar. Inventor Adrian David Cheok is spearheading the Mixed Reality Lab, which will engage all five senses in a simulated experience through "multisensory Internet communication." This Uranus phase could also take the IoT ("internet of things") beyond the smart house or driverless car. Perhaps we'll trade swiping and scrolling for device-free computing, as our digital gadgets become one with everyday household objects.

Arts & music: A digital revolution.

Time for some protest anthems—and new ways to raise consciousness? With Uranus in Taurus, ruler of the voice and throat, music could replace chanting and shouting. In 1939, Billie Holiday released her haunting "Strange Fruit," an anti-lynching song that reverberated through the airwaves. In 1935, Benny Goodman was the first Caucasian bandleader to hire an African-American musician to be part of his ensemble, beginning the "desegregation" of American music. Artists like Duke Ellington and Ella Fitzgerald (both Taureans!) rose to national fame, their songs helping to popularize—and in some states legalize—jazz.

Fine art, literature and dance will meet community activism and digital media (Uranus' domain), giving rise to stunning and quirky creations. In 2018, British street artist Banksy commanded $1.4 million dollars for the sale of his spray-paint-on-canvas "Girl with Balloon." Shortly after the Sotheby's auction closed, an alarm sounded and the painting began to slip below the frame, shredded by a hidden device operated by remote control. The half-deconstructed piece reportedly doubled in value *after* the partial self-destruction. That's what we call #UranianLogic! ✳

CHIRON IN ARIES

From wounded warriors to no-limits soldiers: Healer Chiron visits Aries from February 18, 2019, until April 14, 2027.

Oscar Wilde once quipped, "To love oneself is the beginning of a lifelong romance." But how many of us actually know what it means to truly *j'adore* me, myself and *moi*? For starters, cue the Whitney Houston and follow up with a Beyoncé-heavy playlist. The greatest love of all will soon be "happening to me" as Chiron—a comet known to astrologers as the "wounded healer"—began a nine-year journey through self-authorized Aries this past April 17, 2018.

According to Greek mythology, Chiron was a philosopher, teacher—and, yes, healer—who, ironically, could not heal himself. Chiron's placement in our natal charts, as well as its transits, can reveal a core wound that may take a lifetime to work through. But don't stress! Chiron is also a secret power. As you grapple with pain, you gain wisdom that you can pass on to others like a magical salve. In fact, the symbol for Chiron is shaped like a key since unlocking his powers opens up a portal to deep, inner peace.

Chiron orbits between two intensely oppositional planets—uptight, restrictive Saturn and liberated, revolutionary Uranus. His role as the metaphysical mediator can help us synthesize the energy of both. Where do we hold ourselves back (Saturn) and

CHIRON IN ARIES: TOUR DATES

Due to several retrogrades, the comet will weave in and out of Pisces and Taurus during this Ram-bunctious transit:

Apr 17, 2018	Aries
Sep 25, 2018	Retrogrades into Pisces
Feb 18, 2019	Aries
Jun 19, 2026	Taurus
Sep 17, 2026	Retrogrades into Aries
Apr 14, 2027	Taurus

where can we be destructively rebellious (Uranus)? We must understand both extremes in order to find the middle ground. In *Astrology and the Rising of Kundalini*, author Barbara Hand Clow refers to Chiron as the "rainbow bridge" between Saturn and Uranus. Aptly named, since integrating the full spectrum of emotions is the key to wholeness.

While Chiron generally stays in one zodiac sign for eight years, when he enters Saturn's orbit, he can buzz through a single sign in under two years. (It's up to him whether he wants to undergo outpatient surgery or opt for a longer course of therapy.) Since Chiron takes approximate 49 years to journey

through all twelve zodiac signs, we all go through a "Chiron return" around age 50. At this point, core wounds may rear up for another round of cosmic therapy, especially if we've resisted doing any deeper self-examination.

Of course, there's always farther to go! Between ages 49-51, the Chiron return will certainly insist upon soul searching. If we've "done our work" we may be called into leadership roles that allow us to spread our wisdom and flex our healing gifts at this time. Chiron was last in Aries from 1968 to 1976.

Transiting Chiron sets the tone for universal healing: What wounds do we, as a world, need to deal with together? Take a look at Chiron's most recent journey through spiritual, esoteric Pisces—the water sign that rules healing and escape—that began in April 2010. The wellness movement is having a heyday now, from the popularity of juice bars and yoga studios to Oprah's *Super Soul Sunday* and guided meditations with Deepak Chopra. Shamanic healings, like ayahuasca and other sacred medicine ceremonies, are as prevalent in Brooklyn apartments as they are in Peruvian jungles. Whole Foods, once a boutique health food store, is now owned by the behemoth Amazon.

> **"Where do I belong? Do I even need or want to fit in?" We'll all be grappling with identity while Chiron transits Aries.**

Simultaneously, we are painfully present to the shadow of Chiron in Pisces, which also rules institutions like jails and hospitals, and governs our addictive tendencies. From privatized prisons to a distressed health care system to an opioid crisis, there are still wounds to be (ad)dressed! On a worldwide level, we'll all be grappling with identity while Chiron transits through Aries.

Where do I belong? Do I even need (or want!) to fit in? How can I maintain my individuality and *be part of a group?* If you're a Type A overachiever who can't leave the house without your brows on fleek and your outfit styled to Level: Paris Fashion Week, get ready for an existential crisis.

But don't freak out! It's long overdue. Before you can speed down the self-esteem superhighway you have to pass a toll booth guarded by your own inner critic. When the Snapchat filters are off, what voices come up in your head? Getting acquainted with your own self-deprecating thoughts is the way to neutralize them so you can replace them with empowering affirmations.

Warning bell: The goal of Chiron in Aries is not to achieve a narcissistic swagger of, "I'm a queen, get out of my way...I'm doing me!" Rather, think of the next nine years as a beautiful opportunity to understand (and love!) every voice that makes up the chorus of your personality. Are you going to let the tone-deaf-but-eager alto sing the solo aria during a performance at The Met? Heck no! But you're not going to kick them out of the choir, since you know that turning up the volume on other "singers" will integrate him into the composition that is you. In the sage words of Lao Tzu, "Because one accepts oneself, the whole world accepts him or her."

Interestingly, Chiron was originally classified as an asteroid but has gone through an identity crisis of his own. He's now considered a Centaur—part of a class of bodies orbiting between the asteroid belt and the Kuiper belt—and has been leveled up to "minor planet" status while simultaneously being categorized as a comet. Meanwhile, there are talks of calling him a dwarf planet, like his bro Pluto. But whatever his planetary pedigree, understanding his influence can be downright medicinal.

Rugged individualism, which has long been the mantra of the Western world, could hit its limit as oceans are polluted with plastic packaging, greenhouse gases threaten to melt the polar ice caps and the economic divide widens. While "Mine!" might be Aries' favorite word, Chiron in Aries will push for innovation instead of overconsumption. Rather than crowding racks with excessive merchandise, savvy retailers may soon allow shoppers to customize items on the spot through 3D printing and high-speed knitting machines that are gaining popularity in Japan.

Put down those VR and AR glasses—those are *so* Chiron in Aquarius and Pisces. The wounded healer's tour of physical Aries will make RR (reality-reality) en vogue! Instead of living vicariously through YouTubers, we anticipate a resurgence of live events like open-mic nights, interactive sports... or perhaps another upgrade to the Escape Rooms that Chiron in Pisces popularized.

The Ram is also an aggressive warrior, but with Chiron traversing this field, time's up on the "fight or flight" mentality. Drawing guns, dropping bombs, putting up our dukes...the world can't handle much more of that. Chiron in Aries is here to heal the "wounded masculine" which has fueled centuries of bloody destruction and devastation.

Simultaneously, Chiron in Aries may also reveal where a fear of conflict is keeping us stuck in self-destructive patterns. Yes, there's a time to fight for our rights—but is there a way to do so that doesn't involve domination, violence, one-upping and power-mongering? The inquiry begins! ✳

THE 12 SIGNS

ASTROTWINS

IN 2019

SCORPIO
2019 HIGHLIGHTS

LOVE

This year brings an interesting mix of stability and surprises to your love life. Growth-inducing Jupiter in your second house of security helps you see the magic in the mundane. Sharing the little things can feel like an adventure, and single Scorpios may be drawn to someone you'd previously overlooked as "boring." But with radical changemaker Uranus in your relationship house, partnerships might be shaken, not stirred. You could be drawn to a wildly different type of person or you might crave more autonomy in your ties. Even if you end up in something super-steady, you'll find a way to keep things from getting too predictable!

MONEY & CAREER

This could be one of your luckiest money years in over a decade, as abundant Jupiter visits Sagittarius and your second house of work and finances until December. You might relocate for a job, get a plum promotion or start an entirely new career. But you can build a steady nest egg with consistent saving, conscious spending and by putting a bit more away each week, no matter what your income. In January, a final Leo lunar eclipse may bring an exciting leadership opportunity or clarity around your path. A new series of Cancer/Capricorn eclipses could bring unexpected writing, teaching or media projects.

HEALTH & WELLNESS

In March, destabilizing Uranus exits your health and wellness zone, not to return again in your lifetime. Any fluctuations in your sleep, eating or exercise cycles could taper off, and you'll find it easier to stick to routines. With disciplined Saturn in your mindful third house, pay attention to what you feed your head this year. As the saying goes, "thoughts become things," so keep the negative self-talk at bay with affirmations, personal growth workshops and inspiring books and podcasts.

FAMILY & FRIENDS

The planets hold a cosmic convention in Capricorn and your social third house this year, which could bring new friendships and community involvement. You might immerse yourself in local events, perhaps taking an official role in your neighborhood or school district. With serious Saturn and transformational Pluto here, it's all about who you know, so be selective about the company you keep. Do your friends lift you up or drag you down? Distance yourself from the needy ones and surround yourself with go-getters. ✳

SCORPIO
2019 HOROSCOPE

2019 POWER DATES

SCORPIO NEW MOON
October 27

SCORPIO FULL MOON
May 18

SUN IN SCORPIO
October 23–November 22

Park the tour bus, Scorpio: Your reinvention headliner is wrapping up! Last year, you embarked on a new decade-plus chapter of your life as expansive Jupiter plunged into Scorpio from October 10, 2017, until November 8, 2018—its first visit to your sign since 2006. Jupiter only visits your sign every 12 years, bringing massive growth and evolution, if not a complete 180-degree flip. As 2019 begins, your whole life may look wildly different than it did a year ago.

Novelty and new experiences are awesome, but have you had a little too much of a good thing?

Last year, many of our Scorpio friends moved, got married, launched businesses and began exploring entirely new paths. It was a lot of change, especially for a strategic sign that likes to feel in control and plan ahead!

This year, energy downshifts to a more practical and grounded groove, as Jupiter will spend the bulk of 2019 in Sagittarius and your second house of security, money and routines. Now, you can figure out where to direct all the new energy—and begin building your wild ideas into something concrete. You'll have a chance to integrate and process

everything that came flying at you. If you planted new seeds, you can sort the crops and decide which ones are keepers.

Jupiter is the planet of extreme growth, so hosting it in your sign— your first house of self and identity— can be exciting and exhausting in equal measures. On the one hand, lucky Jupiter's auspicious influence helped you make a powerful fresh start in places where you've been stuck forever. (Yay for leaving the sordid and painful past behind!) But still—you're a calculating and control-loving sign, Scorpio.

> "Hosting Jupiter in your sign can be exciting and exhausting in equal measure."

Jupiter's concentrated energy bursts made it hard for you to plot anything too solid since plans were subject to change without notice. You had to be spontaneous and leap without a safety net. The whole "starting fresh" thing, as lovely as it sounds in an Instagram meme, may have arrived on the heels of a painful disappointment or loss from the year prior. Many Scorpios spent 2018 in a state of "cognitive dissonance"—fumbling around trying to get your bearings in a strange new reality.

Last year was especially intense because the eclipses—powerful lunar forces that sweep in and bring sudden change—have been touching down on the Leo/Aquarius axis since February 2017, shaking up your home, family and career sectors. You may have moved, changed jobs, become a parent or stepped into hefty new responsibilities

at work. Parent-child relationships were also dramatically impacted by the eclipses, and you may have stepped into a totally new role in your family.

As if that wasn't enough, radical Uranus jumped into Taurus and your relationships sector for the first installment of an eight-year visit that only happens every 84 years! From May until November 2018, Uranus turned your interpersonal ties upside-down. Your entire approach to partnership got a radical revamp, one that will continue for a longer stretch (until 2026) beginning this March. Uranus is taking one last lap through Aries and your sixth house of work and wellness until March 6, wrapping up an eight-year cycle that's brought shifts to your routines since 2011. After that, Uranus will depart this sign, and won't return again until next century!

Either way, the stars seemed hell-bent on reinventing all the most important areas of your life at once in 2018. Luckily, Scorpio is the sign of extremes and you don't tend to do anything halfway. But you do prefer to have that happen while you're in the driver's seat! For the last couple years, you've been a passenger on the universe's extreme Uber ride, with no idea of your final destination. There was no time to prepare, and while you've become amazingly resilient from adapting and bouncing back, this is not your preferred way to travel through life!

Good news: In 2019, you'll not only get your bearings, but you'll finally be able to throw down a few anchors. Jupiter will spend nearly the entire year (until December 2) in Sagittarius and your stabilizing second house, lending life a much more measured pace. It will be more like a gentle Sunday drive through the country—or a butter-smooth ride in a luxury E-class sedan—than a reckless high-speed chase. You'll be focused on taking calculated risks, growing your nest egg and enjoying the simple pleasures of life more fully. New money-making and work opportunities could arrive, and auspicious Jupiter will boost your self-confidence.

The very last Leo eclipse arrives on January 21, finishing off a two-year cycle of work-life rebalancing. This lunar (full moon) lift could bring one last round of career changes, which may include a prestigious offer or a chance to finally be recognized for your expertise. After that, the eclipses will spend the next couple years touching down on the Cancer/Capricorn axis, a much gentler process that could bring thrilling opportunities to travel, teach, study and shift away from outmoded thought patterns.

This divine directive to "express yourself" will be echoed by a pileup of planets that are visiting Capricorn and your third house of communication and community all year. Structured Saturn is spending its second full year here, helping you find (and refine) your voice and build a solid platform for your message. And transformational Pluto will continue its 16-year journey through Capricorn that's spanning from 2008 to 2024, reshaping the way you think, speak and share. If you've been hiding your brilliance, you could finally get the courage to share your visionary ideas with the world, especially in December, when outspoken Jupiter starts a yearlong visit to Capricorn, punctuated by a Capricorn solar eclipse and a once-every-35-years meetup of Saturn and Pluto.

Whew! The second decade of the twenty-first century will not go out quietly—and especially not for you. Get ready for an innovative start to the new decade as the calendar turns. Your friendships, beliefs and interests could look rather different from the way they did ten years ago…or even ten months ago. Move forward confidently, trusting that your savvy ideas, intellect and wits will guide you to the right connections and opportunities!

Jupiter in Sagittarius: Prosperity and security.

November 8, 2018–December 2, 2019

Can routines and consistency create more freedom in your life? In 2019, the answer is a resounding "Yes!" Adventurous Jupiter spends nearly the full year in Sagittarius and your second house of work, money and security, which could make 2019 one of your most stabilizing and profitable years.

The quickest path to abundance is to set your priorities and stick to them. Less is more this year, so don't try to be a jack-of-all-trades, or scatter yourself among too many projects. Define your lofty vision, then break it down into simple action steps you can take every day. This is the year to do the work—to draft the plans, build the foundation, walk the talk. The second house rules daily routines and habits, and with twinkly-eyed Jupiter sprinkling

SCORPIO

pixie dust on your life, you'll find the magic in the mundane this year. Sink your teeth into a big project, like a home renovation or something meaty that needs your dedicated time and attention.

With Jupiter in Scorpio for most of 2018, you threw the metaphorical spaghetti against the wall. Now, Jupiter will reveal what sticks. One of those "noodles" (or zoodles, if you prefer) could turn into a highly successful and lucrative opportunity.

"One of your ideas could turn into a highly successful and lucrative opportunity. "

One friend, an aspiring writer who worked in IT, decided to finally write a novel while Jupiter transited through her second house a few years ago. She set a goal of writing three pages per day and did that—even if a lot of those words didn't make the final cut. Some days, she wrote brilliant passages, other days produced near-gibberish, but it didn't matter. The point was to build the muscle of consistently producing written work, instead of just dreaming about it. As the saying goes, "Writers write." By the end of the Jupiter transit, she had a finished manuscript to shop to agents.

Another friend used this Jupiter transit to build his passion project: a catering business specializing in healthy, handmade empanadas. During this Jupiter transit, we watched him determinedly turn a clever idea into a brick-and-mortar shop. He started by selling small quantities of empanadas at healthy and gourmet delis in New York city, then served them at food festivals and buzzy parties, becoming

known as the "empanada guy." He then created a pop-up shop in his native Bronx, which launched to such excitement that investors started circling. He leveraged that into a long-term lease that became his "empanada lab"—which doubled as a community upliftment space with hands-on classes for local youth, live music and, of course, empanadas. It's the perfect example of how hustling with a singular mission can pay off while Jupiter's in your corner.

Jupiter only visits this part of your chart every 12 years, and its last visit to Sagittarius was from November 24, 2006, to December 18, 2007. Look back to that time, if you're old enough to remember: Did you start a new job or career path? Was there a moment when you found your footing, or made a decisive choice to take a different life direction? Maybe it was one of your more anchoring years, when you stayed put and "poured the concrete" rather than gallivanting to glamorous events around the globe.

As Jupiter starts a new 12-year phase for your work and finances, you may feel like a chapter of your career is coming to a natural transition point. Are you ready for a promotion, to develop new skills, or even to pursue a whole new direction? This is the start of the next 12-year phase for your work life, so don't be afraid to take a leap of faith and stretch beyond the familiar. You could also become a savvy student of budgeting, saving, planning and building

39

a nest egg…or more of one than you already are! Although Scorpio rules the zodiac's eighth house of investing and passive income, cash is king while Jupiter visits your second house of earned income. Think long-term and short-term, and keep some money in the bank. Become a better steward of your day-to-day earnings and a conscientious consumer. Under wise Jupiter's influence, you might even end up teaching or coaching others to create success, using your own life as a template. Working with a pro mentor can transform your approach to finances, too.

Jupiter rules long-distance connections, entrepreneurship and higher education. Some Scorpios could relocate for a job opportunity or take a position that involves travel and lots of video-conferencing across time zones. Maybe you'll be tapped to open your company's new international office (a year in Barcelona or Buenos Aires doesn't sound too shabby, does it?) or outsource to offshore service providers. With Jupiter's entrepreneurial bent, you might start constructing the foundation of your own venture. If you're a business owner, this could be one of your most profitable years, when your balance sheets appear in Scorpio's favorite color: black!

Since the second house rules self-worth, buoyant Jupiter here can bring a major confidence boost. You start to believe in yourself and recognize that your contributions are valuable. The more you invest in

Numero Uno, the less you care what anyone else thinks about your choices. That's called "healthy self-esteem," Scorpio, and you'll get a megadose of it from Jupiter. Whether you're negotiating a raise, setting firm boundaries with family or asking for what you need in love, Jupiter reminds you to keep yourself in the equation.

Your love life will also benefit from Jupiter's stabilizing touch. For single Scorpios, this is the year you could meet the person you marry—or at least, someone who's marriage material. While Jupiter transits this security-minded zone, people you overlooked as "boring" or "too quiet" will actually seem like a good catch. You're interested in character, not just what's on the surface or their credentials. And you'll leave the fairytale romance to other people (who needs to slay dragons and escape doom just to have a damn dinner date?). In 2019, ain't nothing like the real thing, baby. Instead of dreaming about fur-lined handcuffs or installing a sex swing in the bedroom, you may start envisioning matching Adirondack chairs on the porch as you watch your children and grandchildren grow up. (We kid…but not entirely!)

For couples, this is a lovely year of appreciating the little things. All those small moments add up to the big love story, and Jupiter in your sensual second house really helps you savor each moment. That will be a lovely change for a sign like yours that's famous for obsessing about the future! Enjoy

> **"People you overlooked as 'boring' or 'too quiet' could actually seem like a good catch."**

being in a comfortable groove with your beloved, instead of fixating on where things are going. Since the second house rules practical luxury, book some classy date nights—or a trip where you totally spoil yourselves, since worldly Jupiter loves to play travel agent.

Although you're primed for smart money moves, there are a few times this year when Jupiter will lock into a conflicting square (a 90-degree angle of tension) with nebulous Neptune, which is in your fifth house of love, passion and decadence. Temptations could topple your disciplined efforts, or you might recognize a need to build more fun and pleasure into your routines. The Jupiter-Neptune squares will be on January 13, June 16, September 21, but you'll feel their dynamic tension for all of January and from June through September, as they travel at a close degree to each other. Watch for self-delusion and even outright denial as these two over-optimistic planets can make even a Scorpio turn gullible—no easy feat! You may be torn between dueling desires for security and excitement, so work out the right ratio for yourself.

Jupiter in Capricorn:
Bring your message to the masses.

December 2, 2019-December 19, 2020

What's the big idea? Well, it's probably one of your visionary concepts, which you'll get especially psyched about at the end of this year. In December, Jupiter will join structured Saturn and transformational Pluto in Capricorn, bringing a

playful and outspoken touch to your third house of communication. This could give you the "urge to purge" before the calendar turns, either to get a lot of pent-up stuff out in the open or to really start sharing your ideas with the world. You've been hammering away at these plans for a few good years, and it's time to start road-testing them on the public.

As a business coach once said to us, "Done is better than perfect." If you're obsessively trying to tweak or self-edit your concepts before you release them, it's time for a new approach. Roll things out in phases, do surveys, do live gatherings to let people sample the flavor. Think in bite-sized morsels, not giant, irreversible moves. With knowledge-loving Jupiter in this curious sector, it's a great time to sign up for classes, devour books, listen to webinars and get your hands dirty trying new things. After a busy year with Jupiter in your work house, you're ready for more playtime—namely, intellectually stimulating hobbies and fun DIY ventures.

The third house rules siblings, friends and community, and these could be major growth areas as you draft your New Year's resolutions. Ready for a big change of location in the new decade? With expansive Jupiter roving through your third house of neighborhoods, you might start exploring new districts—if not to move, maybe to set up a business or to find new social outlets. Move past the same old hangouts and refresh your "favorites." Over the next 12 months, you might hop between cities or check out a new town for a possible relocation. Our advice? Try before you buy. Rent an Airbnb for a week to see what it really feels like living there. Go to the cafes, take a yoga class, visit the schools

if you have kids…run through your usual routine and see how it translates into real-time. Maybe that adorable little beach town or big city you glamorized is actually best left as a favorite vacation spot, not a permanent home.

With Jupiter in this variety-loving sector, it's all about exploring your options and creating a bounty of choices. Don't lock yourself into anything too permanent. Next December, when Jupiter moves into Aquarius and your fourth house of home and roots for a year, you can funnel all that research into more permanent accommodations or lifestyle changes.

Saturn in Capricorn: Aligning thought, speech and action.

December 19, 2017-December 17, 2020

Your words and thoughts shape your reality, a truth you've grown familiar with in the past year. In 2019, structured Saturn will spend its second full year in Capricorn and your third house of communication, prompting you to get serious about what passes through your Scorpio filters. What things do you repeat to yourself silently, even when you're not aware you're doing it? What conversations do you engage in regularly with friends and family? Do you even know?

Negative self-talk and limiting beliefs can have a far-reaching effect, even on our health. The field of epigenetics is showing how we can switch certain genes on and off, short-circuiting some of our predisposition to aging and disease through food, environment and exercise. But those choices begin with our thoughts and emotions, which you're learning to navigate skillfully now. You might check out Dr. Joe Dispenza's books Becoming Supernatural and You Are the Placebo, along with his meditations and workshops, to learn more about how our unconscious thoughts can cascade us down a rabbit hole of unwellness—or completely alchemize everything. As the sign of transformation and power, it should be good news that you can learn to control and conduct your own DNA's symphony!

The third house rules siblings, neighbors and friends—the people who are around you a lot of the time—and serious Saturn's got you being more selective about the company you keep. Are they forwarding your goals or dragging you down with drama, bickering and gossip? While that stuff can be addictive, your desire to waste precious minutes on the hottest piece of water-cooler intel is evaporating by the second.

More than anything, you crave ambitious people who are up to important things—role models and no-nonsense types. Business expert and gazillionaire Jim Rohm's theory was that your net worth is the average of the five people you hang around the most. Whether or not it's true, this Saturn phase, which will last on and off until December 2020, is reshaping and refining your inner circle. Combine work and play by networking or socializing for a purpose.

Saturn is also recrafting the way you show up in your friendships and relationships. Do you bite your tongue instead of speaking up? Now, you'll get the temerity to ask questions and voice your opinions with a sense of authority. If you end every sentence with a question mark, it's time to own your voice! You might even benefit from working with a vocal coach or getting media training. Or, if you're the icy and intimidating type of Scorpio, you might learn to communicate more effectively (e.g., with words instead of your classic "death stare").

The third house rules writing, teaching, media and local activity. Do you have a book or an app idea brewing? Serious Saturn can help you learn the nuts-and-bolts process of making your dream a reality or pitching a solid idea to investors. The third house rules elementary education, so if you're a parent, you could run for the school board or PTA, or become an advocate for improvements in your district. You might take a leadership post in your neighborhood (Mayor Scorpio…or perhaps a seat on the Chamber of Commerce?).

Do you dream of working for yourself—or are you a business owner? Start small and in your own backyard, and soon you'll grow a healthy "garden" for your ideas. Think: tables at festivals and street fairs, pop-up shops or hosting events in your 'hood. If your audience is more of a "psychographic," then you could give an online workshop teaching a specific skill. This is your year to build a platform and learn some of the 101 basics of marketing. Lock in that domain name and play around with some of the WYSIWYG website builders like Wix and Squarespace.

Even though we now live in a social media-driven world, the rules of human psychology haven't changed—and they're something that your sign innately grasps. Take a few courses to boost your credentials and know-how so you can reach people through more channels. Old-school Saturn doesn't want you to change your message—just add a few more mediums so you can spread it farther.

Saturn Meets Pluto:
Metamorphosis.
December 2019-February 2020

Saturn is all about bringing the unseen into tangible form, and when it makes a once-every-35-years meetup with your ruler, shadowy Pluto, from December 20, 2019, until February 5, 2020, some of your most ancient fears and beliefs could reveal their origins. That could bring a rare opportunity to let go of blocks and anxiety for once and for all. Ready to break free from your own mental prison? Saturn helps you follow a step-by-step process, preferably guided by a trained expert.

You could be connected to life-changing books, teachers, workshops and podcasts during this time. Or, you might just create your own inspirational and educational products, especially ones that share a story of triumph and transformation over impossible odds. How did you rise from the ashes, like your symbol the phoenix, and fly free again?

The AstroTwins' 2019 Planetary Planner

Uranus in Taurus:
Revamp your relationships.

March 6, 2019-April 26, 2026

Do your relationships feel like they're running on autopilot? Are you having the same conversations you've had millions of times or lapsing into small talk? Mix it up, Scorpio! This March, radical changemaker Uranus will start an eye-opening eight-year visit to Taurus and your seventh house of partnerships, completely renovating your interpersonal ties. Your approach to relationships—and the way you interact with other people—could make a total 180-degree turn. Small talk will give way to #RealTalk, as you seek authentic connections where people's individuality is celebrated, not scorned or suppressed.

With unconventional Uranus here, you might explore new ways of partnering, both in work and love, where you write the rules, rather than following a tired old script. Uranus is the planet of sudden changes, and you could spontaneously enter—or exit—a serious relationship in the next few years. If you're in a stable long-term duo, you might completely uproot your shared lifestyle, or you'll just crave more autonomy. This is the kind of cosmic transit when, say, a couple who's been together for years decides to live in separate homes, tries an open relationship or sells their suburban digs to hit the road in an Airstream trailer.

Some of your choices might stun people, but with shock-jock Uranus in charge, being true to yourself is more important than what any outsider thinks.

Maybe you'll just get a little more open-minded in your love life. As the saying goes, monogamy doesn't have to equal monotony!

Single Scorpios could explore a new style of relationship, or you might meet a promising match online, since Uranus rules technology. Many Scorpios we know like to keep a low profile in the digital realm—if they're even on social media at all. Now, you might lift your ban (or at least, soften it). This is especially true in December, when Uranus will form a helpful trine (a harmonious 120-degree angle) to expansive Jupiter in your third house of communication and community. Proactively use the digital domain to connect to your tribe and link up with like-minded people—for work, love or to collaborate on a pioneering project.

You got a sneak preview of this last year, because Uranus made a brief pit stop in Taurus from May 15 to November 6, 2018. After that, Uranus backed into Aries and your orderly, health-conscious sixth house for a final visit, reminding you to get your affairs in order before you get too enmeshed with someone else. This March, Uranus will settle into Taurus for a long stretch, revamping your relationships until April 2026. Uranus only visits each sign every 84 years, making this a literal once-in-a-lifetime transit for most Scorpios (its last visit was from 1934 to 1942).

Disruptor Uranus doesn't arrive gently, though—especially because Uranus is in "fall" in Taurus, its least comfortable sign to visit. It makes sense: Uranus is the planet of radical change while Taurus is all about consistency and stability. There can be a bit of a "midlife crisis" vibe to this transit, especially

if you've suppressed your individual needs for the sake of a relationship or friendship. Expect to feel the tectonic plates shifting as Uranus liberates you from those codependent or imbalanced ties.

Uranus is one of the slow-moving outer planets, so its influence spans a longer portion of our lives, and also shapes a generation. The celestial shock jock's mission is to help you become more upfront in all your interpersonal dealings—to thine own self be true. By doing so, you may lose a few "user-friendly" folks, but you'll quickly fill those seats with people who celebrate the real you.

Someone you wrote off as "weird" in the past might turn out to be an amazing ally or a way-shower who introduces you to a mind-blowing new perspective. Or, you could team up with someone who's outrageously different from you, forming an unlikely but attention-grabbing dynamic duo. Think beyond the familiar when it comes to partnerships in 2019.

Final Leo Eclipse:
Rising to the top.

January 21
Your turn to lead, Scorpio! On January 21, your ambitions surge skyward as a Leo total lunar eclipse lands in your tenth house of career and public acclaim. This is the grand finale of an eclipse series that's been touching down on the Leo/Aquarius axis since February 2017, transforming your personal and professional paths. Home, family, career and status have been majorly reworked by the hand of

these potent eclipses. Perhaps you've reimagined your whole work-life balance (whatever that is these days!), moved to a new address or changed career paths. Relationships with parents and children have also been remastered by these eclipses.

Look back to the two prior Leo lunar eclipses on February 10, 2017, and January 31, 2018, as they set the stage for what could occur now. If you've been trying to nail down your professional calling or clarify your highest purpose, prepare for another eye-opening round of discoveries. Some Scorpios might make a radical U-turn, quitting a job suddenly or leaving an entire industry. A career that wasn't a good fit could be "eclipsed" away through, say, a departmental restructuring or a company closing. Should this happen, trust that the stars are lining up something much better suited to your strengths. A high-profile opportunity may arise out of the blue, one that could come with new responsibilities, clout and an upgraded income bracket. Carefully consider any offers that arrive near this date. While they might require some adjustments to your lifestyle, the growth opportunity could be well worth it.

Cancer/Capricorn Eclipses:
New conversations, fresh perspectives.

January 5, July 2 & 16, December 26
Has your lens on life gotten too narrow…or maybe a little bit smudged? Four of this year's five eclipses

will touch down in Cancer and Capricorn, activating your axis of communication, community, travel and expansion. Everything is up for questioning under these analytical and philosophical eclipses, which are part of a series running from July 2018 until July 2020. Over the next two years, you might radically change the way you talk, think and interact. If indeed our thoughts create our realities and our conversations shape our beliefs, expect to become hyper-vigilant of the connection between your words, thoughts and deeds!

If you don't like the way something is going in your life, examine what you're saying about it—what do you tell other people and yourself? Do you complain, or maybe sugar-coat a problem, then stew inside? Change the conversations and you could create an entirely new outcome.

The old saying "think globally, act locally" may ring true in 2019, since only one of the eclipses—a July 2 Cancer solar (new moon) eclipse—will hit your ninth house of travel, long-distance connections and risk-taking. While this unpredictable eclipse could bring an opportunity to see new parts of the world or return to school, you might also have an a-ha moment about your greater life purpose. Look back to July 12, 2018, when the very first Cancer solar eclipse first set off this energy wave. A visionary idea that got piqued a year ago could start to become a reality.

But maybe you'll test out that grand vision on a smaller or local scale first? The three Capricorn eclipses will activate your third house of community, socializing and self-expression. It starts with a January 5 Capricorn solar eclipse, which will

travel close to structured Saturn, prompting a hard look at how you interact with others. Are people misinterpreting your intentions, perhaps seeing you as intimidating or hard to read? Maybe it's time to make a conscious change.

You could also get serious about crafting and delivering a message, perhaps through tangible channels like social media, a website or in-person events. You might explore new living arrangements or neighborhoods in earnest. A friendship could turn into an exploratory business partnership. Take it slow and team up on a small project to test the waters.

On July 16, a Capricorn lunar (full moon) eclipse could bring an a-ha moment about your social circle, community and the way you express yourself. If there was ever a day to come out with a bold message, it's now—and it could be a transformational one, since alchemist Pluto (your celestial ruler) will be hovering nearby. Given Pluto's penchant for secrecy, you might want to create a dramatic air of mystery or build excitement that leads up to a grand debut. Work those "teasers" and drop hints to get your audience eager for the unveiling (or to press "buy now"!). Karmic Pluto could connect you to a kindred spirit at this eclipse, someone you feel like you've known for lifetimes—and maybe you have. This person could play a critical role in your development over the next year.

On December 26, a second Capricorn solar (new moon) eclipse arrives—this one an annular eclipse, also known as a "ring of fire" because the Sun's rays will peek out from behind the shadow of the moon, creating a flaming outline. At this point, Jupiter,

Saturn and Pluto will all be in Capricorn—and Saturn and Pluto will be merging their energies—which could create a powerful moment to speak your truth or have a life-changing dialogue.

Chiron in Aries:
Healing perfectionism and control issues.

February 18, 2019–April 14, 2027

It's no secret that your sign likes to be in control, but has your need for the upper hand passed the healthy load limit? On February 18, Chiron, the comet that's now considered a minor planet, starts an extended voyage through Aries and your sixth house of health, organization and order.

In Greek mythology, Chiron was the "wounded healer," a philosopher and teacher who could help everyone else but couldn't fix his own issues. Chiron reveals how we can heal others through doing our own deep inner work. Chiron was already briefly in Aries from April 17 to September 25, 2018, and in 2019, it will settle here for a longer trip, staying until April 14, 2027.

If you suffer from debilitating perfectionism (or deflecting that by being excessively critical of others), Chiron will teach you tolerance. For the next eight years, your transformational journey could involve learning to play well with others. But before that can happen, you'll need to identify the roots of any struggles. Perhaps you've shielded yourself from pain by always having the answers.

But you can only carry so much weight on your own shoulders, Scorpio. Delegating —to the right people and with the right systems in place—could be part of your learning curve.

Chiron will reveal where you may have picked up trust issues, perhaps from a critical parent, teacher or caregiver. That could manifest as body image issues or an inability to relax and receive. If your health goes through any bumpy patches, look to the mind-body-spirit connection. Chiron could be pointing toward a core wound that's manifesting as a physical condition. Louise Hay's classic book You Can Heal Your Life has a fascinating list linking emotional blocks and physical symptoms. You might radically change your diet, fitness or sleep habits, then go on to share your transformative wellness journey with others. This Chiron phase could teach you healthy coping mechanisms for stress—starting with finding a proper outlet for yours, rather than holding it all inside. ✳

MONTHLY HOTSPOTS

JANUARY: LOVE HOTSPOTS

January 7-February 3: Venus in Sagittarius

As the amorous planet cruises through your zone of money and stability, you might feel that the hottest quality in a love interest is their ability to give you a sense of comfort and security. For the next four weeks, you're more into easy companionship than boudoir gymnastics. With beautifying Venus in this posh and polished zone, a style overhaul and some much-needed pampering could get you in the mood for love.

January 13: Jupiter-Neptune square

In lust we trust? Eager Jupiter and gullible Neptune make their first of three clashes this year (the next two are on June 16 and September 21), tempting you to overturn your hard-won stability in pursuit of passion. Since both of these planets are known for being unrealistic and overshooting the mark, this impulsivity could backfire. Since, like Oscar Wilde, you "can resist everything except temptation," impose a couple limits on yourself. The ultimate goal is to create a love life that brings both spontaneity *and* predictability—a hard act for even the most well-matched couples to pull off!

January 18: Venus-Mars trine

With the love planets mashed up in your most grounded houses, you'll be in sync with your mate or, if, you might actually enjoy the dating game! Love won't feel like a competition, and you'll both relish building a bond that makes you feel more connected.

January 20: Venus-Neptune square

You love them, you love them…notsomuch? As Venus in your security-seeking sector clashes with gullible Neptune in your lusty fifth house, your own wandering eye could destabilize a connection, or you may catch a case of "grass is greener" syndrome.

January 22: Venus-Jupiter meetup

As the "benefics" (positive, helpful planets) unite in your most stabilizing sectors, you're more interested in a love match with "marathon" potential than a short-but-sweet sprint. Couples should do something a bit upscale tonight and savor the luxury. Single? Take a gamble on someone who may seem a bit restrained but gives off a vibe of sensuality and adventurousness.

January 24-February 10: Mercury in Aquarius

Sharing is caring, Scorpio, so let down your heart wall and open up at least a little about your feelings. Not only is it okay to be vulnerable, it's what makes you human—and attractive!

JANUARY: CAREER HOTSPOTS

January 2: Sun-Saturn meetup

Err on the side of "talk less, listen more" today as the self-assured Sun gets humbled by restrained Saturn during their once-a-year conjunction. Give an older, wiser or more experienced person the floor before you rush in with an answer. Since this celestial summit is in Capricorn and your communicative third house, you may second-guess the merit of one of your ideas. It seemed brilliant a few days ago but might only get a lukewarm reception. Don't beat yourself up. Instead, sit with the feedback and apply some of it to make your concept even tighter.

January 4: Mercury-Uranus trine

Rules *are* made to be broken, and under this golden mashup of the celestial innovators in your grounded houses, it'll pay to be a bit of a maverick. To solve a troublesome problem, you'll need to approach it from a *very* different angle. Don't sit there staring at the screen or spreadsheet. Get out and wander, and let inspiration find you.

January 4: Capricorn new moon (partial solar eclipse)

The annual "time to sow" new moon in Capricorn and your collaborative corner lays the groundwork for big things to come over the next sixth months. And, because it's a solar eclipse that falls in close proximity to Saturn (which rules Capricorn), this one has the potential to turn into something major. Stay tuned…and be patient.

January 4-24: Mercury in Capricorn

Analytical Mercury's transit of your cerebral corner turns you into a veritable ideas machine. Come out of your cubicle to brainstorm with colleagues and explore creative synergies. Pro tip: Always show up at meetings with tons of questions prepared —an easy task for your penetrating mind, Scorpio.

January 6: Uranus retrograde ends

All systems go! Wonky Uranus ends a five-month retrograde that made it hard to stick to a system or routine. If you were job searching, there could have been one false lead after another. As Uranus powers forward in Aries and your organized sixth house, you'll be able to gain traction. Look outside the usual avenues, since innovative Uranus could bring leads from unexpected sources. And if all else fails, Uranus will exit Aries on March 6, not to return again this century. You might spend the next couple months getting your skills (especially technology) up to speed for your industry.

January 8: Mercury-Mars square

What's worse than a know-it-all? A know-it-all who also loves to argue. You might encounter one of these unpleasant types today, so be prepared. And if they happen to be trying to sabotage you at a meeting or playing extreme devil's advocate, come prepared with all your facts and figures and be ready to fight back with a bulletproof case. Some-

times being challenged is a blessing in disguise because it pushes you to not coast.

January 11: Sun-Pluto meetup
Have that capture device at the ready—or maybe plan a Live social media event for today. You'll be so "on" it's not even funny! Under this once-a-year mashup of these potent planets in your communication corner, you'll have the knowledge *and* gift of gab to move the masses.

January 13: Mercury-Saturn meetup
Don't rush to share an idea before it's 100 percent ready—and even then, you might want to go back and give it one last coat of polish. While Mercury delivers the brainstorms, conservative Saturn insists that every detail be triple-checked. Nail this, and you might be writing your own ticket!

January 13: Jupiter-Neptune square
The first of 2019's three clashes between overconfident Jupiter and nebulous Neptune could make you impulsive with money, especially if your ego gets involved. Showing off, especially by picking up the tab, might impress someone—but it also plants an expectation that you'll be handling the check from here on out. And you might always wonder: Do they like you for who you are or what you can do for them? Similarly, don't get all impressed by someone else's flash. Make sure there's substance underneath the swagger.

January 18: Mercury-Pluto meetup
Strike a balance between going deep on a research project and keeping things light enough that everyone can follow. If you've got someone onboard who *would* like to take things to the next level, talk it through in detail. Make sure they're actually on the same page and not just trying to impress you.

January 18: Sun-Uranus square
Your ideas are solid, but that's no reason *not* to listen to someone else's. This isn't a zero-sum game. In fact, by combining the best elements of both of your plans, you might wind up with a slam dunk.

January 21: Leo full moon (total lunar eclipse and supermoon)
This powerful supermoon and lunar eclipse is the grand finale in a series of eclipses that fell on the Leo/Aquarius axis between February 2017 and now. Look back to the previous Leo lunar eclipses (February 10, 2017, and January 31, 2018) for clues and cues about what this might bring. Hint: Don't abandon your loftiest goals, however "unrealistic" they may seem. Remember, Scorpio, where others see obstacles, you see only possibilities.

January 21: Mars-Saturn square
You don't have to speed up to keep pace with others today, especially if you feel like they're moving too fast for you to keep your clarity about your piece of a project. That said, if you need more info or explanation, don't just fumble your way through. There's no shame in asking smart questions!

January 23: Mercury-Uranus square
The only thing you can count on today is unpredictability, so try to stay flexible and don't lock into anything too definite. People might change their minds or simply refuse to commit. Rather than get frustrated, focus on what you can do all by yourself.

January 24-February 10: Mercury in Aquarius

A little personal touch will go a long way in dealing with clients and colleagues over the next two and a half weeks. With the communication planet touring your sensitive fourth house, you'll feel more connected to coworkers and will actually be interested in their personal lives—to a degree. Just make sure you have healthy boundaries in place so you don't encourage an oversharer!

January 25: Mars-Jupiter trine

Take a chance on…something! As go-getter Mars forms a cooperative trine to expansive Jupiter in your money and work sectors, the right combination of risk-taking and knowing your stuff could bring in a big win. As the saying goes, luck is where preparation meets opportunity—and those words ring oh-so-true today.

FEBRUARY: LOVE HOTSPOTS

February 2: Venus-Uranus trine

Newsflash: You don't have to be in control 24/7. Loosen up on the reins and let someone else call the shots or—here's a radical notion—support *you* for a change. Single? Stay open to serendipity. You could meet a great person when you least expect it today.

February 3-March 1: Venus in Capricorn

Talk is sweet! As Venus shimmies into your social third house, conversation is an aphrodisiac. Couples get back in sync with common interests and lively outings, so be spontaneous. Your flirt factor hits peak levels—right in time for Valentine's

Day. With Cupid's arrows aimed at your immediate circle, a friend may start to look fetching.

February 4: Aquarius new moon (Chinese New Year)

A heart-opening moment arrives as the Aquarius new moon beams into your sentimental fourth house. Talk could turn to moving in together, making babies or meeting each other's families in the coming six months. Today also kicks off the Chinese Year of the Earth Pig, a sensual and decadent cycle. Turn your home into a haven where you can really let your hair down!

February 10-April 17: Mercury in Pisces

The expressive planet will take an extra-long vacation in your romance sector due to a retrograde from March 5 to 28. Things should start to pick up speed before then, but if they slow down (or go MIA) during that time, be patient. This could be a lesson in taking your time to get it right!

February 14-March 31: Mars in Taurus

When passionate Mars returns to your relationship house for the first time in two long years, you'll be more than ready! For couples, this can bring a resurrection of desire or renewed intensity about your commitment. Just watch for competition or buried resentments to arise. Single? Make the most of this generous opportunity by going out more, chatting up interesting people and being more liberal with your right-swiping.

February 18: Venus-Saturn meetup

This serious sync-up sets the stage for an important conversation or invites you to take a longer view

about your romantic future. If you've been holding something inside, this is a perfect day to express it—calmly, keeping your own fear or anger in check.

February 19: Mercury-Neptune meetup

A boundary-dissolving mashup of mental Mercury and dreamweaver Neptune in your fifth house of amour can be great for your romantic life—if you can keep both feet planted on terra firma. It'll be easy to get caught up in a fantasyland. But keep it real and you might experience an almost telepathic connection with someone.

February 22: Venus-Pluto meetup

Interpersonal interaction can get hot and heavy under this intensifying mashup. But if that's exactly what you've been craving, then initiate a conversation in which you speak from the heart—and encourage your love interest to do the same. Just make sure you're prepared for anything!

FEBRUARY: CAREER HOTSPOTS

February 1: Mars-Pluto square

This overbearing clash could leave you in a state of analysis paralysis, and while you like a good challenge, you *don't* enjoy being overwhelmed. What to do? For starters, stop multitasking and just focus on one thing at a time. And when strong emotions come up, resist the urge to lash out at someone or post a rant on social media.

February 10-April 17: Mercury in Pisces

Your brainstorms could start to gain serious traction in the next few weeks as mental Mercury thunders through your creative fifth house. This is an extra-

long cycle because of a retrograde from March 5 to 28, which is good news (more time to get this idea off the ground!) *and* bad because retrogrades bring delays and confusion. What to do? Get going now, then work behind the scenes while you wait out the retrograde next month.

February 13: Mars-Uranus meetup

When motivator Mars connects up with disruptor Uranus—something that only happens once every other year—there's no predicting what will happen, but you can count on it being a game-changer. With these two cosmic catalysts in your sixth house of work and service, you might get tapped to do some high-profile work that helps others. Don't overthink this; just say yes!

February 14-March 31: Mars in Taurus

When dynamic Mars blasts into your partnership zone for the first time in two years, a deal, contract or collaboration could get fast-tracked. Be ready to spring into action, even if you've been twiddling your thumbs for weeks. With the red planet in the sign of the steadfast Bull, any offers could have longevity.

February 19: Virgo full moon (supermoon)

A team project you've been working on—or trying to get invited to participate in—hits a turning point today. What can you contribute that's uniquely you? Don't be shy about volunteering. And if this work can help an important cause, all the better!

February 22: Mercury-Jupiter square

Listen to that little voice inside your head today, even if the rest of you is eager to dive in. Under this tense cosmic clash, things might not be as they

appear: Someone could be holding back a key piece of intel that'll be a game-changer. Rather than rush in, prepare a lengthy list of questions…and fire away!

MARCH: LOVE HOTSPOTS

March 1-26: Venus in Aquarius

You'll be hankering for homespun vibes as Venus makes her annual visit to your sentimental fourth house. Don't fight any waves of nostalgia that rise up on your emotion ocean. This period of domesticity could spark discussions about moving in together, family plans or how you're both really feeling.

March 1: Venus-Uranus square

It might not be easy to put your own complaints or arguments aside under this testy cosmic tiff, which can cause people to act rashly or make knee-jerk decisions. One of you might be digging in your heels, leading to a battle of wills that no one wants. Hard as it is, listen to the other person's point of view and do your best to not be defensive. If you can think of anything that might help, suggest a compromise.

March 5-28: Mercury retrograde in Pisces

An amorous interlude may get interrupted today as expressive Mercury reverses course in your romance sector. If you rushed into something, this could have a positive, tempering effect, but if Mercury invades a blissful bubble, you might not be so pleased. Practice patience. This is a chance to review imbalances and help get things on a more even keel. For some Scorpios, Mercury's pivot could

rekindle an old flame. Just be careful if you're going to play with fire!

March 6: Pisces new moon

Stay open to something new and out of the ordinary under the year's only new moon of fresh starts in your passionate fifth house. Looking to change things up? This lunar lift can help—if you're ready to shuck an old habit or limiting belief that's held you back. Singles could have a new relationship status by the end of the month; and couples may get serious about intense subjects like family planning—or expanding!

March 6, 2019-April 26, 2026: Uranus in Taurus

Your approach to relationships will undergo a dramatic sea change starting today, as disruptor Uranus kicks off an eight-year visit to your partnership house. You got a sneak preview of this last May 15 to November 6, but then the cosmic transformer shifted into reverse. This time it's here for the long haul, not to return for another 84 years. You can look forward to meeting some intriguing new characters who can shift the way you view interpersonal dynamics. Spoiler alert: You may be challenged to look at any control issues in a whole new, liberating light!

March 14: Mars-Saturn trine

When passionate Mars in your eighth house of eroticism and intimacy meets up with stability-minded Saturn in your house of emotional security, trust is more important than lust. You won't be satisfied with a fling and will be looking for something with real potential. Under this straight-talking mashup, you'll be able to discuss your

 The AstroTwins' 2019 Planetary Planner

desires from a more self-aware place, which is an important starting point!

March 20: Libra full moon and supermoon

This first of two back-to-back full moons in Libra and your introspective twelfth house dials up your intuition, especially in a key relationship. You may suddenly "know" it's time to allow someone to get closer or, on the flip side, be ready to cut the cord. Since the twelfth house rules transitions and healing, you'll have all the cosmic support you need.

March 20: Mars-Pluto trine

Under this deepening alignment of your two celestial rulers, you'll feel an almost preternatural bond with someone. But don't keep it to yourself! Reach out and spend time together today or at least hold a marathon phone session in which you bring up a subject you've been afraid to broach. If you speak from your heart, they'll be sure to hear you loud and clear.

March 21: Venus-Mars square

Pulled in two directions much? Today's confusing skies might find you equally eager to dive into a new relationship *and* keep it casual. You can blame the conflict-addled angle between Venus in your intimacy zone and Mars in your platonic HQ. Is this something you can simply stall on? Coupled Scorpios could have mood swings today. It would be so easy to take that out on your partner, but resist the urge. Not everything comes out in the wash.

March 24: Mercury-Neptune meetup

In a rerun of February 19, these two starry-eyed planets meet again in your romance house—and this time, mental Mercury is retrograde. What may seem realer than real could actually be a projection of your desires, and even those could change in a few days when Mercury turns direct. Enjoy the dreamy vibes, but don't get into anything you can't easily and painlessly get out of!

March 26-April 20: Venus in Pisces

With the love planet cruising through your passionate fifth house for the next three and a half weeks, you might have a one-track mind. This can be a great time for couples to deepen your bond and for singles to double down on your dating efforts. But keep it light, let things flow—and enjoy the ride!

March 28: Mercury retrograde ends

Love, actually? As communicator Mercury ends a three-week backspin through your passionate fifth house, the drama dies down and confusion clears. Single Scorpios can ease back into the dating game and couples will find it easier to settle any recent misunderstandings or disagreements.

March 31-May 15: Mars in Gemini

When lusty Mars returns to your eighth house of sex and intimacy for the first time in two years, you'll remember what real passion feels like. While your sign is a magnet for intensity, make sure you're not confusing lust for love. Of course, if you don't really care about the difference, ignore that last suggestion!

MARCH: CAREER HOTSPOTS

March 5-28: Mercury retrograde in Pisces

When the communication planet shifts into reverse

in your creativity sector, your big idea might not hit the mark. Don't push too hard, and don't take it personally. Go back to the drawing board with an open mind and let new notions come (they will!). Watch out for anyone on an ego trip who might try to "kick you while you're down." If you don't let them, they can't hurt you!

March 6: Pisces new moon

The year's only Pisces new moon activates your fifth house of creativity and self-expression. Invest in your talents, whether you're a neophyte signing up for lessons or a pro who's ready to put your gifts on display. Start building a platform, booking gigs or scouting performance spaces.

March 6, 2019-April 26, 2026: Uranus in Taurus

After a brief visit to your partnership zone from May 15 to November 6, 2018, the radical innovator turned retrograde and focused your attention on wrapping up some lingering personal issues. But when it returns for a long cycle starting today, you'll have several years to find suitable collaborators and business partners to help you launch an ambitious project. Whether this is part of your "day job" or a start-up idea of your own, you'll be able to slowly but surely gain traction. Taurus energy is all about taking one methodical step at a time and not quitting 'til you reach the finish line!

March 6: Sun-Neptune meetup

Don't overthink it, Scorpio: If there's something you've been eager to test-drive, just hit the gas and see what happens. When these two cosmic idealists meet up in your creativity corner today, they can give birth to true genius!

March 13: Sun-Jupiter square

Not every day is going to light your fire, but are there little things *you* can do to keep your motivation high? Challenge yourself to work just a little harder or to add some bells and whistles to a presentation. Finding small ways to push yourself can make you even better at your job *and* bring a spirit of playfulness to your work.

March 14: Mars-Saturn trine

Steady, strategic moves could seal a major deal or win you a crucial ally. With cautious Saturn and courageous Mars syncing their superpowers in your interpersonal zones, set your sights on exactly what you want—then pounce!

March 15: Mercury-Jupiter square

Be careful not to promise more than you can deliver today, which will be all too easy with analytical Mercury in an overreaching square with idealistic Jupiter. Step back and reevaluate the situation. People will still respect you if you come back with a more realistic estimate—in fact, the smart ones will have even greater veneration for your honesty.

March 20: Libra full moon (supermoon)

The first of this year's two back-to-back full moons in your twelfth house of transitions helps you see a situation for what it is and not what you'd like it to be. You may have to say no to a work offer or change your role on a team, but if it makes you happier—and more productive—then it's worth it.

March 20: Mars-Pluto trine

Come out and say it! With your ruling planets in perfect harmony, you'll have the insight *and* the confidence to voice what everyone's thinking but

no one's willing to utter. Make sure you're being as thoughtful as you are strategic, and you'll be sure to win a few new fans. Working on an important negotiation? Push just a little harder and it might blast forward now.

March 31-May 15: Mars in Gemini

As driven Mars returns to your eighth house of long-term finances and joint ventures for the first time in two years, you may be seeing a partnership or investment in a whole new light. Talk to the necessary people to implement any changes that are needed, and don't second-guess yourself!

APRIL: LOVE HOTSPOTS

April 10: Venus-Neptune meetup

Under the alignment of these dreamy planets in your romance zone, it'll be easy to get swept away by fantasy—whether it involves a flesh-and-blood love interest or not. While a little rosy-eyed optimism can be a good thing, confusing reality with a projection isn't. Enjoy the feel-good vibes but know who (or what) you're actually dealing with.

April 15: Venus-Jupiter square

You might have to make a tough choice between steamy adventures and commitment under today's tug-of-war. Of course, you'd love to have both, but if you're not willing to let your partner play on a longer leash (or go totally off-leash), you can't expect to be able to have *your* fun. Single? Be clear about what you're looking for: That's exactly what you'll attract!

April 19: Libra full moon

The second of two rare, consecutive full moons (the first was March 20) in your twelfth house of closure and fantasy could spark a soulmate connection or open your eyes to where denial has permeated your life. If you've been unsure whether to stay or go, this full moon can help you decide.

April 20-May 15: Venus in Aries

Amorous Venus puts down roots—at least for three and a half weeks—in your pragmatic and organized sixth house. If you've been dating up a storm, pull the emergency brake and get a handle on what you want in a partner (or if you even want one). Unsure where things are headed with your longtime lover? Slow down and talk through your relationship goals to determine whether you're still on the same page.

April 22: Sun-Uranus meetup

This once-a-year mashup can be a game-changer: Whether that's a good thing or not depends on how honest you've been about your emotional needs. As the liberated disruptor of the zodiac, Uranus can force you to face some inconvenient truths… and because it's aligned with the ego-driven Sun in your partnership zone, you might need to let someone know what's really in your heart.

April 27: Mars-Neptune square

If you're getting a strange feeling about someone you're involved with or interested in, don't ignore it. Your Spidey senses are generally spot-on accurate, and by following up with some pointed questions, you can get to the truth pretty quickly. Just bear in mind that this emotional mashup in your passionate houses can spike your jealousy, paranoia and attraction to the "dark side."

56

APRIL: CAREER HOTSPOTS

April 5: Aries new moon

The year's only new moon in trailblazing Aries powers up your sixth house of healthy and efficient living. Are there a few simple changes or life hacks you can do to make your routine run more smoothly or productively? Over the next two weeks, clear out any clutter, organize your workspace and pare down your schedule. While you're at it, how about getting a bodywork appointment on the books?

April 10: Sun-Saturn square

If someone can't seem to make a decision on something you're waiting for, take advantage of that "bonus" time by hunkering down on a project of your own that you can knock out of the park all by yourself. And make sure you're poised to blast ahead when you *do* get that green light!

April 10-August 11: Jupiter retrograde in Sagittarius

When larger-than-life Jupiter flips into its annual four-month backspin, make sure your spending isn't outpacing your earnings. It's easy to shell out money without a thought to your budget, but eventually that's going to catch up with you. Before you make *any* purchases, make sure it's something you truly need (or desperately want). And even then, do some research to guarantee you're getting the best possible price!

April 12: Mercury-Jupiter square

Be careful not to slip into oversharing territory today. This "information overload" clash of the communication planet and supersizer Jupiter can loosen the very lips that sink ships. Before you put anything into production, go back and check it!

April 13: Sun-Pluto square

This is not a good day to negotiate any important deals or try to engage anyone in the kind of discussion that "should" lead to a compromise. With these power-tripping planets at loggerheads, people will be defensive and unwilling to yield even an inch. Save your energy for next week.

April 17-May 6: Mercury in Aries

Analytical Mercury sails into your practical, organized sixth house for its annual tour de force, helping you focus on those annoying yet essential tasks that keep your life running like a well-oiled machine. This is also a great time to start paying more attention to your health. But think in terms of adding more positive habits, not what you have to "live without." Deprivation never works!

April 19: Libra full moon

Do they have your back…or are they out to stab you in it? The second of two rare full moons in Libra (the first was a month ago) and your twelfth house of illusions can reveal who's really on Team Scorpio and who's just an opportunist.

April 22: Sun-Uranus meetup

Swallow your pride and invite someone to help you on a pet project. But don't join forces with a person who thinks the exact same way you do. A complementary talent, not a clone, will help you take this to the next level. And if they're an outlier type, even better!

April 24-October 3: Pluto retrograde in Capricorn

Be prepared for miscommunications and scrambled signals—yes, for five-plus months—as your co-ruler, shadowy Pluto, shifts into reverse in your third house of expression and community. Plan to be even more exact in your instructions and put *everything* in writing. It can't hurt to go over the most important things with people multiple times—until you're confident they get it.

April 29-September 18: Saturn retrograde in Capricorn

As if a retrograde Pluto in your communication house weren't frustrating enough, today cautious Saturn begins *its* five-month backspin in this same important realm. Watch for sarcasm and other accidental intensity in your expression. And be extra discerning about what you share on social media. Something you consider innocent can come back to haunt you.

MAY: LOVE HOTSPOTS

May 4: Taurus new moon

The year's only new moon blazes into your relationship realm, bringing fresh-start energy to your bonds. Single? Wipe the slate clean and focus on the most important qualities you seek in a partner or lover. The more clearly you can envision it—and the higher you set the bar—the more likely you'll be to manifest your desires. Under this earthily sensual moon, couples can rekindle sparks or take a concrete step to cement your bond, whether "officializing" the union or planning a second honeymoon.

May 6-21: Mercury in Taurus

If you're not in sync with your mate or love interest, you can't expect them to read your mind. (Not everyone's as intuitive as your tuned-in sign!) With the messenger planet breezing through your partnership corner, it's on you to express your feelings—and to listen to theirs!

May 7: Venus-Saturn square

Do your words accurately reflect what you're feeling—*and* your highest values? A little compromise is expected in relationships, but you don't have to shape-shift to fit into someone else's vision of how you or the union should be.

May 8: Mercury-Uranus meetup

In this rare, once-a-year mashup of impulsive Uranus and mental Mercury, you could get a wild hare to make a budding connection more committed—or to end an existing partnership. While it's true that sometimes it's better to just rip off the bandages, you don't want to do anything *too* rash, so think before you act today!

May 9: Venus-Jupiter trine

The sexiest pillow talk for you under this grounding alignment might be a discussion about a shared future. You're feeling good about a union and may be seeking a greater sense of security. How can you combine your resources and talents to be better and stronger together than individually? If you're single, the less you *try* to meet someone, the more success you'll have. Just be you—the friendliest, most outgoing version—and see who you attract.

May 9: Venus-Pluto square

Temper, temper! When shadowy Pluto throws

shade at the love planet, you might feel anger, jealousy or suspicions arise from your gut. But tune in: Just because you're feeling this doesn't mean it's valid. Before you make any accusations, get the whole story. And if a budding love interest turns into a ghost, do *not* pursue.

May 15-June 8: Venus in Taurus

Today marks one of the sweetest cycles of the year as the love goddess pays her respects to your seventh house of committed relationships. Over the next three weeks, you can deepen your bond, get something new off the ground or meet your match. Keep an open mind and be willing to compromise in the name of amour!

May 15-July 1: Mars in Cancer

"Different" equals "hot" for the next month and a half as sizzling Mars blazes a fiery trail through your ninth house of expanded horizons. Chemistry could ignite with someone from a different culture or background from yours. Couples can turn up the temperature by planning a thrilling vacation or diving into a new hobby together.

May 18: Venus-Uranus meetup

Need a relationship reboot? How about a revolution? You don't have to settle for the status quo if it's not bringing you the kind of joy or satisfaction you crave. Even if you're happy (for the most part), you can make some sweeping shifts under this transformative energy. Ready, set, manifest!

May 21-June 4: Mercury in Gemini

Talk dirty to you? As communicator Mercury parades through its "home" sign of expressive Gemini and your eighth house of intense emotions, you

may be inspired to share a secret desire or confess a crush. Attached? No more assumptions: Whatever's on your mind, it's time to finally come out and say it!

May 29: Mercury-Neptune square

The more you dig, the deeper you'll tumble down a (possibly bottomless) rabbit hole. As Mercury in your probing eighth house clashes with nebulous Neptune, attempts to find "evidence"—whether of someone's transgressions or their interest in you—will be a wild goose chase. It's a thin line between perceptiveness and paranoia today. While you shouldn't ignore any nagging feelings, there's a good chance they're coming from past fears, not your current situation.

May 31: Venus-Saturn trine

With amorous Venus in your partnership zone, you're ready and eager to get to know someone better. And with this harmonious mashup to stern Saturn in your communication corner, even your flirting will convey a more serious attitude. Make sure you're representing yourself honestly, because your "bait" will determine what you reel in.

MAY: CAREER HOTSPOTS

May 1: Mercury-Saturn square

What you thought was a slam dunk may turn out to be a shooting error. No moping allowed! Pick yourself up and try-try again. Chances are you'll find the flaw in your idea or design and come up with something *so* much better.

May 2: Mercury-Pluto square

No cutting corners today. The last thing you want

The AstroTwins' 2019 Planetary Planner

is for someone else to find a glaring error in your work, so take the time to go back and review everything with a fine-toothed comb. Hold others to this same exacting standard, because their work will reflect on you.

May 2: Mercury-Jupiter trine

Open up your thinking to include some options that didn't initially feel right. With expansive Jupiter high-fiving analytical Mercury in your practical houses, you can apply your incisive thinking to a wider range of possibilities and, in the process, hit on a brilliant solution!

May 4: Taurus new moon

This annual lunar lift in your partnership zone gives you the confidence to approach an individual or small group about joining forces on a project close to your heart. If you're already part of a professional team and not 100 percent satisfied with the dynamics or results, the next two weeks are perfect for expressing your concerns—diplomatically, of course.

May 5: Mars-Jupiter opposition

Taking a small, calculated risk could be a smart idea—but betting the farm on an unproved notion is not! Your normal cautiousness may be MIA today as these two adventurous (and sometimes reckless) planets oppose each other. Look, listen, consider… but hold off on acting!

May 6-21: Mercury in Taurus

Another wave of cosmic support arrives as the messenger planet kicks off its annual tour of your dynamic-duos realm. Speak now, Scorpio…or you may be stuck holding your piece!

May 8: Mercury-Uranus meetup

A budding alliance could come together fast as verbal Mercury aligns with impulsive Uranus in your partnership zone. But take time to do the necessary background checks, including references and financials. You can't build up without a solid foundation.

May 11: Sun-Saturn trine

Curb your enthusiasm today! Even with the self-assured Sun forming a supportive angle to reliable Saturn in your "people" houses, someone might not be showing all their cards. Better to take a slow and cautious approach in all your business dealings. If something *is* the real deal, you'll find out soon enough—and with plenty of time to pursue it.

May 13: Sun-Pluto trine

By being an active listener (i.e., engaged but silent) today, conversations will flow easily and you'll be able to reach an agreement that had eluded you last week. But while you're tuning in, focus on people's body language and what they're *not* saying if you want to get the whole story.

May 15-July 1: Mars in Cancer

Driven Mars returns to your expansive ninth house for the first time in two years, helping you overcome your resistance and take a risk on something you really want. This is also the most candid part of your chart, and with the hot-blooded planet here, you may surprise yourself with what comes out of your mouth!

May 16: Mercury-Saturn trine

You love the idea of teaming up with successful people, but make sure they share your values and work ethic. Under this productive pairing, you

could launch a powerful partnership, so take the necessary steps to get that creative ball rolling.

May 18: Scorpio full moon

Rise and shine! This annual full moon in your sign redirects your attention to an important project. It's easy to get caught up in work goals and the company's objectives, but you have a say in what you spend your time doing. This lunation asks: How can you blend your personal talents and professional drive and *really* make a difference?

May 18: Mercury-Pluto trine

Rally the troops and have a face-to-face (even if that happens on video conference) to make sure everyone's still on the same page. With a big project, it's easy for people to veer off in divergent directions. Under this incisive starmap, sit down and have a strategy meeting. If you need to do any negotiating, this is a good day to advance your cause.

May 21-June 4: Mercury in Gemini

Sharpen your focus! Today kicks off a two-week period when your mind is like a laser. What important project have you been procrastinating on, waiting for a burst of mental clarity? Shuffle your priorities and have a go at it. Don't underestimate your formidable abilities!

May 29: Mercury-Neptune square

Don't let drama derail your agenda. Sure, a coworker might be going through a crisis in her love life, for example, but unless you're being paid to be her life coach, you've got work to do! At the same time, don't be *so* tunnel-visioned that you come across as cold or uncaring. Either make plans to discuss personal stuff over lunch or, if you're not interested in that, explain that you are "really busy" so they take their problems elsewhere.

May 30: Mercury-Jupiter opposition

Keep it real! It'll be easy to be carried away by your projections today as analytical Mercury gets blown off-course by larger-than-life Jupiter across your financial axis. Double-check your numbers and consider having an actual accountant or financial planner review them for you. Also, watch the urge to drop big bucks on an impulse buy.

JUNE LOVE HOTSPOTS

June 2: Venus-Pluto trine

Still waters run oh-so deep. Today, as romance-minded Venus in your partnership sector hooks up with probing Pluto, you won't be happy with anything superficial. Whether you're single or attached, you're seeking conversations that stir the deepest levels of your psyche. Been dying to share a secret desire? Spill it!

June 3: Gemini new moon

The year's only new moon in your eighth house of eroticism and intimacy kicks off a six-month cycle for finding or deepening a love match. "Dark" moons bring opportunities for fresh starts, so if you're hoping to mix things up, start now. In the sign of gregarious Gemini, conversations could become your favorite kind of foreplay!

June 8-July 3: Venus in Gemini

When amorous Venus skates into your eighth house of intimacy and merging, your words and deeds will carry more weight—and be packed with seduc-

tive power. If you've been keeping people at arm's length, look at why. Is fear holding you back? The only way to overcome that is to get back on the horse that threw you. Couples should spend more quality time together—in and out of the boudoir!

June 14: Mars-Neptune trine

Today could wind up being one of the most fantasy-fueled days of the year, ripe for a spring fling that might turn into a summer romance (and beyond!). Just be true to what you really desire. If you're playing for keeps, don't settle for a player. Attached? Let the combo of dreamy Neptune and red-blooded Mars in your adventure zone help you mix things up.

June 16: Jupiter-Neptune square

As the second of three clashes occurs between these two unrealistic planets, you could attempt to rush into (or out of) something serious in the throes of emotion. An all-consuming attraction could overtake you, sending common sense right out the window. If you're looking for excitement, there are ways to get it without destabilizing your hard-won security. The first of these rare Jupiter-Neptune squares was on January 13 and the next is on September 21, but you'll feel these dueling desires for passion and predictability for the next three months as the two planets will travel in close proximity all summer.

June 21-November 27: Neptune retrograde in Pisces

Love, actually? As illusion spinner Neptune reverses gears in your fifth house of romance for five months, you could have second thoughts about an attraction or a budding connection. An ex could resurface, tempting you to "go there" against your better judgment. Couples should be extra mindful not to get snared in drama. Gather the facts before you react.

June 23: Venus-Jupiter opposition

You love the heady rush of new love (or lust), but under this larger-than-life alignment, you could become overwhelmed by emotions. You don't mind getting a little lost in fantasy, but you need to know what's real…and someone's intense come-ons could make that impossible. Hit pause and try to get clarity before you do anything impulsive.

June 24: Venus-Neptune square

Mind the line between innocent crush and unhealthy obsession, which could get a little blurry under today's fantasy-laced starmap. Enjoy the attention and feel-good vibes, but don't let yourself slide down a slippery slope. Attached? Rather than let yourself become consumed by locking down a commitment, enjoy the sweetness you have in the moment.

JUNE: CAREER HOTSPOTS

June 3: Gemini new moon

How open are you to different ways of making money? Challenge yourself under this fresh-starts lunation by considering a whole new approach to joint ventures and investing. Just because you never tried something doesn't mean it can't be successful now. That's what new moons are all about!

June 4-26: Mercury in Cancer

Today marks the first of the messenger planet's two

trips to Cancer this year (it will return during a retrograde next month, staying from July 19 to August 11). As creative Mercury wings through your expansive, visionary ninth house, you'll be able to shuck off some old habitual ways of thinking and take a wider, wilder, more optimistic perspective. Here's to blue-sky dreaming!

June 10: Sun-Jupiter opposition
Keep a tight grip on your wallet today—and pay attention to underlying feelings that might tempt you to overspend or be inappropriately generous with people you don't know well. Be honest with yourself? Are you using retail therapy to fill an emotional hole, impress people or win someone's affection? Jupiter can overinflate your confidence now, but at the end of the month, you alone are going to have to pay that credit card bill!

June 14: Mars-Saturn opposition
Don't be too quick to make your big reveal. Even if you're totally stoked about an idea, not everyone is going to see eye-to-eye with you—and that could crush your enthusiasm. With buzzkill Saturn raining on passionate Mars' parade, mull this over for one more day or until you're 100 percent sure it can fly. Better safe than sorry.

June 16: Mercury-Neptune trine
Creativity can be your access to the divine, and with clever Mercury and spiritual Neptune united, your grand visions could actually be channeled downloads. Don't dismiss any whimsical or "out there" ideas today. Dare to think big, bold and outside the box. Feeling blocked? Listen to music or a guided meditation, or do your work anywhere but at the office. Who says you can't bring a laptop to your favorite art museum or answer emails from the beach?

June 16: Mercury-Saturn opposition
Big ideas won't fly unless you also pay attention to the little details. With glib Mercury in your visionary zone opposing structured Saturn, you'll need to back up those lofty concepts with solid data and a well-crafted plan, especially if you hope to get a green light from decision makers.

June 16: Jupiter-Neptune square
The second of this year's three clashes between bombastic Jupiter and naïve Neptune could find you playing fast and loose with your money or gambling on a creative but risky concept. The first of these squares was on January 13, so look back to that date for clues of what might resurface now. Jupiter and Neptune will remain at odds for the next three months, coming to a third and final confrontation on September 21. Between now and then, explore how you can make money from your passions without breaking the bank or find the right balance of security and spontaneity. A calculated risk or a small investment in one of your imaginative ideas might pay off—but you'll have to be patient!

June 17: Sagittarius full moon
Bring on the abundance! Today's full moon in optimistic Sagittarius and your second house of work and money bodes well for your financial health over the coming six months. But this doesn't mean you should sit around waiting. Pursue job leads, consider launching a sideline business, or talk to a financial planner about making your income and investments work harder for you.

June 18: Mercury-Mars meetup

Ready, set…hey, where did you go? Today's over-zealous conjunction of idea maven Mercury and impatient Mars activates your restless ninth house. You could move from idea to execution at warp speed. But wait—did you skip a few steps here? Don't tamp down your enthusiasm, but keep things in the blue-sky visioning phase for now.

June 19: Mercury-Pluto opposition

Loose lips not only sink ships, they could provoke a tsunami. With chatty Mercury in your outspoken ninth house, you might be tempted to let your un-filtered opinions rip. But thanks to an opposition from shadowy Pluto, your words could be used against you. Make sure your audience can "handle the truth." And think twice before posting anything too edgy on a public forum. You never know how people will interpret things these days—and even if you mean well, you don't need those words coming back to haunt you.

June 19: Mars-Pluto opposition

With your celestial guardians at odds today, you could clash with someone over your visionary plans. Make sure you have adequate data and solid enough projections before you even present these to the world. On the flip side, if you feel like someone is putting pressure on you, don't think twice about asking for a little more time.

June 26-July 19: Mercury in Leo

No one's questioning the brilliance of your idea, but now comes the hard part: creating an appropri-ate structure. You don't have to do this by yourself. Enlist a team and take your time getting this right.

The messenger planet will be retrograde from July 7 to July 31, which includes a backroll into Cancer on July 19, so set things in motion and stay on top of it, but give your end goal ample time to come together.

JULY: LOVE HOTSPOTS

July 1-August 18: Mars in Leo

Fixated on the future? Mars spends the next few weeks heating up your tenth house of long-term goals, setting your sights on some clear-cut roman-tic goals. Just make sure that it doesn't turn into an obsession, since single-minded Mars can transform you into a bulldozer. Couples could feel pressure to take the next step, or you might argue about what you want for the long haul. Hey, better to get it out in the open, even if there's some short-term ten-sion. With the lusty red planet in your career zone, a workplace attraction could heat up. Sparks may fly with someone significantly older or younger than you.

July 3-27: Venus in Cancer

When vixen Venus veers into your borderless ninth house, you won't get snagged by the petty stuff that can derail an otherwise solid relationship. You might not even be deterred by the fact that some-one lives in another time zone or country. Coupled Scorpios: How far have you gotten on planning that romantic summer getaway?

July 11: Mars-Uranus square

Don't let work demands destabilize your partner-ship—or your quest for one. There *is* a way to keep these things in balance, but it takes effort. If your

partner or love interest is suddenly acting erratically, don't react in kneejerk fashion. Request a sit-down and hash it out before it gets out of control.

July 17: Venus-Saturn opposition

If you rushed into an affair without taking the time to really get to know someone, today's speed-checking face-off between amorous Venus and highway patrol Saturn may slow your roll. While your first reaction may be frustration, stop and look for the silver lining. Maybe you *are* going too fast? Even couples might need to backtrack on a plan that wasn't well thought out enough.

July 18: Venus-Neptune trine

The real world can wait. This dreamy mashup of the love planet and fantasy-fueled Neptune is a rare and special event, and frankly, you'd rather get a little lost here than labor in so-called reality. Even if you're only indulging a fantasy, relish the joyride—just make sure you can follow the breadcrumbs back.

July 21: Venus-Pluto opposition

Defensive much? Today, as manipulative Pluto in your communication corner shoots a harsh beam to affectionate Venus, you might feel threatened and, as a result, blurt out something in anger. While it might be understandable, it may not be appropriate. If you owe someone an apology, do it quickly—and sincerely.

July 24: Mercury-Venus meetup

Today's stars present the perfect opportunity to hatch some dreamy plans for a getaway—either a romantic one with your S.O. or an adventurous one with a single BFF. You're more open to different types when you're away, and a trip with a friend could be better than a dating site!

July 27-August 21: Venus in Leo

What do you want for your future, Scorpio? Today, as the love planet marches into loyal Leo and your tenth house of future planning, take the reins. If you're single, think about what you could do differently to meet more eligible prospects. Since the tenth house is also your career corner, perhaps you've been overlooking the obvious at work? An industry event or conference might just be worth attending; you could end up making a connection that's more pleasure than business!

JULY: CAREER HOTSPOTS

July 1-August 18: Mars in Leo

Hit the gas! Determined Mars returns to your tenth house of professional ambition for the first time in two years. Hello, motivation! You'll be firing on all cylinders, eager to set some new goals and stick a few more career feathers in your cap. Be sure to eat well and get plenty of sleep since the competition—and therefore the pressure—could heat up quickly!

July 2: Cancer new moon (partial solar eclipse)

A partial solar eclipse in your expansive ninth house fills you with lofty ideas for an exciting venture that could blow the hinges off your world. Have you been thinking about launching a business, extending your global reach or doing more work-related travel? All of these get a big "Check!" from this lunar lift in your visionary ninth house.

 The AstroTwins' 2019 Planetary Planner

July 7-31: Mercury retrograde

The messenger planet shifts into reverse in your career corner, which could cause a big project to stall or an offer to be removed from the table. No need to hit the panic button, though. This is a temporary setback and, if you want to look on the bright side, a chance to review everything and see if you can't make even minor improvements.

July 8: Mercury-Mars meetup

You don't get a second chance to make a first impression, as the saying goes. Today, as courageous Mars and articulate Mercury unite in your ambitious tenth house, you could dazzle the decision makers with your clever ideas and unstoppable drive.

July 9: Sun-Saturn opposition

Come to a meeting with several balloons—someone may be intent on popping at least one of them! Before you overreact or take this as a personal attack, stop and consider whether their criticism has any merit. (You don't have to do this in front of anyone.) But be honest: If there is a way you can improve on this, humble yourself and do it. You may wind up owing them a debt of gratitude.

July 10: Sun-Neptune trine

See? That "too crazy to fly" idea is exactly the thing that's needed to take a team project to the next level. Today, with your creative and visionary houses lit up by a golden trine, you may be the hero of the day!

July 11: Mars-Uranus square

Watch your step. You don't want to fall into that snake pit of unmasked competition that someone is insistent on feeding. While you've got your own goals, you know that cooperation—rather than nasty antagonism—is the key to success.

July 14: Sun-Pluto opposition

You'll need more than rah-rah enthusiasm to pull off a big project. Temper your optimism with a healthy dose of realism by giving everything a tough review. You may not get a second chance at this, so make sure you've locked down every moving piece and polished them all to a shine.

July 16: Capricorn full moon (lunar eclipse)

The year's only Capricorn full moon also happens to be a partial lunar eclipse, and because it falls in your communication corner—in close proximity to penetrating Pluto— you'll have people's rapt attention. This begs the question, What message do you want to put out to the world? This lunar lift takes up to six months to unfold, so if you don't have an answer yet, get busy with the take-home part of your quiz!

July 19-August 11: Mercury enters Cancer

Strengthen those filters! Retrograde Mercury will back out of Leo and into Cancer, making a brief second trip this year through your outspoken and expansive ninth house. The quicksilver planet will remain in reverse until July 31, so keep those big ideas (and brash remarks) to yourself until it straightens out. But for the last ten days of this visit, your colorful commentary and insightful advice could be a game-changer.

July 25: Mars-Jupiter trine

C'mon big money! With motivated Mars in your career corner linked up with auspicious Jupiter in

66

your financial sector, today could bring a prolific payout. Make sure you're clear on your goals, then make that big ask, negotiate a higher rate and roll out the welcome mat for prosperity.

July 29: Sun-Uranus square
Ouch! Just as a mission is well on its way to being accomplished, someone's ego trip could threaten to derail it. Don't blindly react to their power plays: Put on your therapist's chapeau and try to get to the underlying motivation. Listening to their ideas might be all they needed in the first place.

July 31: Leo new moon
The new moon in your professional tenth house can help you reach some new heights. But do you have a goal and a game plan? No worries if you don't yet, but over the coming six months, get busy dreaming and scheming. Once you're clear on your objectives, you can begin to manifest them.

AUGUST: LOVE HOTSPOTS

August 2: Venus-Uranus square
Skip the assumptions and make sure you're on the same page for a shared future. With disruptor Uranus throwing a wild pitch at the planet of amour from your relationship corner, it might turn out that someone is getting cold feet. Talk it over before it reaches the point where it's too squirrelly to discuss. Single? Your love of excitement could be interfering with your attempts to secure a commitment. It might be time for some soul-searching.

August 8: Venus-Jupiter trine
Your eyes, mind and heart are all wide open under this expansive alignment of the love planet and optimistic Jupiter in passionate fire signs. This would be a perfect moment to start planning a trip—on your own or with your favorite plus-one.

August 11, 2019-January 11, 2020: Uranus retrograde in Taurus
Just as things are chugging along nicely, the unpredictable planet reverses course in your relationship sector. You or your love interest might have a change of heart, or the union could be straining under growing pains. If one of you is needing more independence, don't hide your head in the sand. Talk about it like two mature adults!

August 15: Aquarius full moon
The annual full moon in your sentimental fourth house could trigger an emotional avalanche that you never saw coming. Go with it, Scorpio (keeping a box of tissues within reach). You might decide to make a real estate move in the coming weeks, or receive major news about a family member, domestic situation or a pregnancy.

August 18-October 3: Mars in Virgo
When the red-blooded planet returns to your eleventh house of friendship and technology, single Scorpios might get some new ideas about where and how (and with whom) to find love. A platonic pal could suddenly be irresistibly attractive: Approach with caution! Download a new dating app and add fresh photos and an enticing profile. Even if you've been disappointed in the past, this is the dawn of a new day! For couples, hosting parties and hanging out with mutual friends will get the

mojo flowing. Head to a concert, festival or sports event—the more novelty and adventure you can introduce, the better.

August 21-September 14: Venus in Virgo

As the other love planet (Venus) joins Mars in your eleventh house, you'll feel optimistic about your romantic future, ready to explore new possibilities. Stay open to different types and look beneath the surface as you get to know someone. Couples will enjoy lighter, more social activities that fortify your friendship. You might even rack up some karmic brownie points by playing matchmaker for a couple of your pals or coworkers.

August 24: Venus-Mars meetup

When the love planets unite, it could be one of the year's best days—and nights—for romancing! Pull out all the stops and trust a gut feeling. This may be a person you've been hanging out with a lot lately, a friend you'd like to extend a benefits package to or someone you "randomly" meet through mutual friends.

August 26: Venus-Uranus trine

Don't judge it; just go with it! Under this capricious coupling, you might feel some undeniable (though surprising) chemistry with someone you've just met. You don't have to mate for life, but if the attraction is mutual, why *not* pursue it? Attached? Strengthen the connection with a little more alone-time. True friends won't mind being rescheduled in the name of love!

AUGUST: CAREER HOTSPOTS

August 7: Sun-Jupiter trine

You're so on today that it's almost unfair to the competition. Step up to the negotiating table and take a stand for an important project. With Jupiter in your second house of finances getting a green light from the confident Sun, you can pursue your goals without feeling money-obsessed. This is *your* future, so you should be self-interested. Looking for a new gig? Don't be shy about tooting your own horn!

August 11-29: Mercury in Leo

Clever and communicative Mercury makes a second (retrograde-free!) trip through Leo and your career-driven tenth house. Plans and professional endeavors may have stalled in July, but with this bonus round of Mercury mojo, the action could pick back up again. Silver lining: The delay actually gave you time to tweak your ideas or consider other options. As a result, your pitches will be more powerful and you won't have all your eggs in one basket—a far stronger position to be in.

August 11: Jupiter retrograde ends

Make it rain! Auspicious Jupiter concludes a frustrating four-month retrograde in your second house of work and finances. The red-spotted giant will propel through this enriching realm until December 2, so if you've got any aces up your sleeve, play them soon!

August 11, 2019-January 11, 2020: Uranus retrograde in Taurus

Under this fickle course reversal, things may not be (remotely) as they seem, and someone might be trying to advance a hidden agenda while acting all team-spirited. It's your job to keep things moving along while regarding everyone with your unique blend of encouragement and skepticism. If an ally starts acting flaky, call them on it immediately!

August 16: Mercury-Uranus square

You know what *you* want, but that doesn't mean others will buy in or support your cause—and that includes your loyal, ride-or-die cronies. Sharp-minded Mercury in your structured tenth house helps you craft a clear, concise plan. But with shock-jock Uranus throwing curveballs from your interpersonal seventh house, you'll need to be alert and adaptable at a moment's notice. No matter how "right" your way is, prepare to bend on a few issues, if only to appease the dissenters.

August 18-October 4: Mars in Virgo

The planet of drive and motivation returns to your house of teamwork and technology after being MIA for two years. A collaboration could pick up speed, and if it's Internet-based, it could take off like a rocket! Check in with your stress levels: While this project may be thrilling, Mars can ratchet up tension so slowly you don't even realize how much you're feeling. Take mini self-care breaks to keep your muscles (and eyes) from getting overly strained.

August 21: Mercury-Jupiter trine

This could be one of your luckiest money days of 2019 as clever Mercury and no-limits Jupiter meld their mojo in the most abundant, successful zones of your chart. Throw your hat in the ring for a leadership role or a promotion. Float one of your strategic ideas by a VIP at work. Announce that you're raising your rates soon—then hold a flash sale for loyal clients and customers and rake in some lovely profits!

August 28: Mars-Uranus trine

A deal or collaboration could heat up fast as speedy Mars and game-changer Uranus join forces in your extroverted houses. You know what *you* bring to the table; make sure the other party has as much to offer.

August 29-September 14: Mercury in Virgo

When the cerebral messenger planet blasts into your eleventh house of teamwork and technology, your ideas might be the most innovative and impressive of 'em all. Don't sell yourself short. You've got a lot to contribute, and people may actually be waiting to see what *you* think before they make their next move!

August 29: Sun-Uranus trine

This needle-moving mashup may land you a spot on an avant-garde team that's working on the kind of thing you've been hoping to get involved in. The key to your success is strategic partnerships, so sniff around and make sure the group you've identified is everything you're hoping for.

August 30: Virgo new moon

The annual new moon in your eleventh house is the cherry on top of a parfait of amazing opportunities that have been falling into your lap for the past week. You're becoming aware of your value as a team player, and this lunar lift could inspire you

to bring your dream project to an investor or developer who can make it a reality. Things will unfold over the coming weeks and months, so don't rush this; get it right out of the gate!

SEPTEMBER: LOVE HOTSPOTS

September 1: Venus-Saturn trine
Come out and say it! If you're expecting your love interest to read your mind, you can expect to be disappointed. Today, as the amorous planet aligns with solid Saturn in your expressive zones, you'll be reminded that direct, honest (and compassionate) communication is always the best way to know what's really going on with someone.

September 2: Venus-Jupiter square
You may keep getting pulled in two directions today—and feel highly confused at that! The love planet in your liberated eleventh house is clashing with free-spirited Jupiter...in your security zone! It's not really a matter of either/or: You want to have your cake and eat it, too. But good luck finding someone willing to allow that double standard!

September 4: Venus-Neptune opposition
Playing a little hard to get is one thing: It preserves an air of mystery and builds excitement. But there's a shelf life to that behavior, and if you're about to exceed it, you might wind up turning someone *off* instead of *on*. It may be worth looking at why you're playing it so cool in the first place.

September 6: Venus-Pluto trine
Swig a cup of courage and initiate that conversation you've been dreading! With loving Venus harmoniously aligned with alchemical Pluto in your communication sectors, you'll have the emotional fortitude to approach an important subject with a person of interest or your longtime love. Single? Don't be too quick to dismiss a connection that starts off with a tepid physical attraction—if you're feeling this person on a soul level, it could be worth exploring.

September 13: Mercury-Venus meetup
In an encore performance of July 24, these two chatty planets align in your social sector—and this time messenger Mercury is moving forward, not retrograde. You might reconnect with someone you met over the summer, or things that stalled with a maybe-lover could pick up speed. As long as you aren't putting a special connection at risk, why *not* pursue it?

September 14-October 8: Venus in Libra
These next three-plus weeks are a good time to go inward and examine your deepest emotions—especially if a romance has been moving at a vertigo-inducing pace. It's easy to get pulled along by momentum, but you want to be sure you're really feeling it. Single? During this mini "spiritual retreat," you could magnetize someone with keeper potential, but you've got to work that Law of Attraction!

September 14: Pisces full moon
Wear your heart on your sleeve! The year's only full moon in emotional and intuitive Pisces illuminates your passionate fifth house. No more hiding your feelings, at least not today. Some powerful confessions could come rushing out, and there will be no stemming the tide. (Well, at least you got *that* out

in the open.) A budding attraction may reach the point of no return. If you're both feeling the love, lean in for that kiss and see where the moonlight takes you.

September 14: Mars-Neptune opposition

Just like too many cooks in the kitchen, too many opinions can leave you confused—and spoil the broth! It's natural to want high approval ratings from your friends about your relationship, but there are so many problems with that! For starters, they don't really know this person or how you two connect. Plus, it's almost impossible for them *not* to project their own beliefs or attitudes (or jealousy) onto you. Bottom line: Close the polls!

September 19: Mars-Pluto trine

Remember that old "If you love someone, set them free" slogan? You might want to pull it out of mothballs today, as your rulers—hot-blooded Mars and alchemical Pluto— harmonize in your freedom-loving sectors. In a LTR? Try giving each other a little more personal space: Absence will make the heart grow fonder and increase your attraction to each other. Single Scorpios may have an immediately passionate connection to someone you meet randomly, and you might not be able to pump the brakes.

September 21: Jupiter-Neptune square

The third and final showdown between these two overconfident planets brings a surge of "grass is greener" syndrome to your love life. It started back on January13, when Jupiter and Neptune first whipped up dueling desires for security and excitement. Ever since the second square, on June 16, you've been trying valiantly to get your thrills with-

out destabilizing a steady bond or falling for a player. Now you'll either feel the crux of this tension or finally crack the code on how to keep the honeymoon vibes going, long after the novelty wears off and "real life" sets in.

September 25: Venus-Saturn square

You may be forced to deal with a challenging situation today, right when you don't feel remotely up to the task. But with reality-checking Saturn facing off with agreeable Venus, you could discover that someone is exploiting your generosity or that you've been refusing to hear what your partner or a love interest is trying to tell you. You'd rather keep the rose-colored specs on than see life for what it is, but when you get repeated, undeniable hints, it'll be hard to keep your head in the sand.

September 28: Libra new moon

The annual "fresh starts" new moon in romantic Libra and your fantasy-laced twelfth house could spark some dramatic events in your love life. You might finally say yes to someone who's been pursuing you—or you could meet someone out of the blue who has "soulmate" written all over them. If you need to cut a cord with an ex before you can truly move on, work with a therapist or healer who can help you let go for once and for all.

September 30: Venus-Pluto square

Pay attention to what people are telling you today, even though your default setting is to zone out, thanks to Venus in your unconscious sphere battling crafty Pluto in your communication corner. Perhaps you're not getting their subtler hints or you need to ask questions instead of assuming you know how they feel. Authentic conversation

can strengthen an important relationship, but you'll need to approach talks delicately.

SEPTEMBER: CAREER HOTSPOTS

September 1: Mercury-Uranus trine
Feeling stymied by a work problem? Take it to the hivemind! You're surrounded by clever, innovative people. All you have to do is ask for an assist, and several of them will be delighted to put their creativity to work. In your outreach, pay attention to anyone you feel a particular click with—this could plant a seed for a future collaboration!

September 2: Sun-Mars meetup
Sometimes your self-contained sign forgets just how much strength there is in numbers. Today, as the generous Sun unites with daring Mars in your collaboration zone, you might intentionally or accidentally team up with some original thinkers who provide a missing puzzle piece or help you take a big idea to the next level.

September 3: Mercury-Mars meetup
Network like you mean it, Scorpio! Today's connection between chatty Mercury and go-getter Mars hits your eleventh house of group action. Whether you're motivating the troops with a pep talk or introducing yourself to kindred spirits at an industry event, your authentic approach will win you fans. A collaboration could pick up steam today—more than you thought possible!

September 5: Mercury-Saturn trine
With clever Mercury and polished Saturn joining forces in your interpersonal zones, your powers of persuasion are cranked up. Even better? Grounded Saturn will help you *not* come across like a used-car salesperson. Arm yourself with some supporting data before you pitch any ideas. The combination of a great concept and solid research—sprinkled with your starry-eyed enthusiasm and passion for a worthwhile cause—will make this irresistible.

September 6: Mercury-Jupiter square
Think back to the events of August 10 and where you might have *almost* hooked someone. Well, today's clash of the same planets gives you another chance at getting through to them. Even better? This time Mercury isn't retrograde. Tweak your pitch, update your information and give it your best shot!

September 6: Sun-Saturn trine
What are you waiting for? It could be that no one is actually planning to come out and ask for your opinion today, and yet you have some very important intel to impart. A union of the confident Sun and grounded Saturn gives you the eloquence *and* the authority to present your ideas in way that will enthrall your audience. Own your power!

September 7: Mercury-Neptune opposition
Fog rolling in? With articulate Mercury opposing befuddling Neptune, this is hardly the ideal day to present your concepts to your crew of collaborators. Do a little creative visualizing and add some artistic touches, like infusing a dry presentation with motion graphics and royalty-free music or telling a heart-stirring story to bring an abstract idea to life. Be careful what you put on social media and the interwebs today. From trolls to catfishers to sab-

SCORPIO

otaging drama queens, the digital realm can be a minefield of manipulators.

September 8: Sun-Jupiter square

Too many big egos in a small group makes it hard to come to an agreement with clients or colleagues. Everyone wants to be a chief, but nobody wants to do the actual grunt work. With your tech center spotlighted, it's a perfect opportunity to update software and strengthen your important passwords. Make sure you save them someplace you'll be able to find them!

September 8: Mercury-Pluto trine

You can read people like X-rays today, as perceptive Pluto and observant Mercury team up in the most social parts of your chart. Use this short-lived superpower to dig deeper into others' motivations and desires. You can draw out so much with curious questions, and before you know it, you'll have all the intel you need. With stealthy Pluto involved, pay attention to what's *not* being said. Body language and other nonverbal cues will reveal a ton!

September 8: Mars-Saturn trine

While today's starmap calls for shrewd moves, some things are better handled by coming out and saying what you mean directly. With forthright Mars and no-nonsense Saturn partnered in your "people houses," certain folks will respond best to clear-cut instructions and requests. Just because *you* can read between the lines doesn't mean everyone else will get the esoteric memo! For optimal results with less insightful types, give it to them straight.

September 10: Sun-Neptune opposition

Rather than fixate on something somebody said, let them know it didn't sit well with you. Just because they dished it out doesn't mean you have to take it! Keep cool but don't mince words. If they're mature and not defensive, they might even appreciate your reaction.

September 12: Mars-Jupiter square

You may have created a whole scenario in your head that's so rich and complex that you're starting to believe it. But today's bubble-bursting face-off may force you to get the real facts about a person or situation. Clear out the smoke and don't be afraid to find out what's what.

September 13: Sun-Pluto trine

Test the waters with a person or small group that you're thinking about teaming up with. By casually floating some of your ideas past them and gauging their reactions, you can get a good sense of how well you'd mesh. At the same time, stay open to what others might be floating themselves. They could be "scouting" you in the exact same way!

September 14-October 3: Mercury in Libra

While you don't want to confuse your dreams and fabrications for reality during this short but intense cycle, getting a little carried away by your imagination can be a good thing—provided you know which realm you're operating in. This is your annual time to recharge your creative batteries and emerge with some brilliant new plans for the rest of the year.

September 18: Saturn retrograde ends

Since late April, structured Saturn been hindering your thought processes as it lumbers backward through your mental third house. Today, the

slow-moving planet resumes forward motion, helping you think strategically and articulate your ideas with more clarity.

September 19: Mars-Pluto trine

Go into "hawk mode" and circle your target before you swoop down on it today. A cunning and calculating alignment between your rulers, warrior Mars and transformer Pluto, calls for major strategizing, especially when dealing with people. If you play your cards right, you could make a direct hit, nailing a key relationship or opening the door to opportunity.

September 21: Jupiter-Neptune square

One last time! Brace yourself for the third and final conflicting square between overreaching Jupiter and naïve Neptune, which pull you relentlessly between hard work and escapism. You're longing for creativity, passion and excitement, but you could undo all your hard-won stability if you go leaping in without a parachute (or a plan!). As much as you don't want to look at things like budgets and timelines, doing so could make or break the success of a project that's dear to your heart. It all started on January 13 under the first Jupiter-Neptune square, then escalated at the second one on June 16. Now the tension that's been building all summer reaches a head. Learn from your previous mistakes and don't overshoot the mark.

September 22: Mercury-Saturn square

Soften your heart or fortify your boundaries? With Mercury in your impressionable twelfth house battling rigid Saturn, you need to ask the tough questions before rushing into anything. But don't be so unyielding that you kill all creativity in the process.

September 26: Mercury-Pluto square

This is one of those rare days when you almost can't be too skeptical—music to your Scorpio ears? But with manipulative Pluto throwing major shade at the messenger planet, it's better to assume the worst than go into something wide-eyed and bushy-tailed. For your part, make sure *you're* being transparent in your dealings. The last thing you want is to be called a hypocrite!

OCTOBER: LOVE HOTSPOTS

October 4-November 19: Mars in Libra

Lust goes underground—and possibly undercover—as passionate Mars burrows into your clandestine twelfth house for its first visit in two years. You could get caught up in a sketchy situation, possibly involving someone who's not exactly single, or you *might* be the one "double-dipping." Even if you're in a solid union, your paranoid or suspicious side may threaten to unravel it. You might want to talk this out with a professional to prevent (or at least minimize) the collateral damage.

October 8-November 1: Venus in Scorpio

Mojo rising! Today, the cosmic vixen brings her dynamic magnetism to your sign for the next three and a half weeks. Your dance card will fill up so fast you'll probably need to create a wait list. But don't let this superpower go to your head. Be kind and modest even as you're giving the head-turners whiplash. Attached? Make time for your other half, who may be missing alone time with you more than you know.

October 12: Venus-Uranus opposition

This one-day wrench-thrower of a transit could have you running for the exit. But unless you're 100 percent sure there's nothing left in a certain relationship, halt! Uranus in your partnership zone is stirring up your need for more breathing room, but that doesn't mean you need to pull the plug. Talk it out and find a compromise that works for both of you. Single? You'll be happier sampling from the buffet table than committing to just one dish (however tasty).

October 21: Venus-Neptune trine

Indulge the feels under today's rare and dreamy alignment. With romantic Venus canoodling with fantasy agent Neptune in your zone d'amour, you'll be irresistible. Whether you're single or attached, glam it up and have some fun!

October 27: Mars-Saturn square

Hitting the gas while pumping the brakes won't get you far! But you may be unsure of where you want to go, and with whom—and how fast—under this befuddling face-off. While part of you wants to soul-merge, another part would rather keep things at a more manageable pace. There's no right or wrong here; just don't send out mixed messages.

OCTOBER: CAREER HOTSPOTS

October 3-December 9: Mercury in Scorpio

When the expressive planet blazes into your sign, you won't have to raise your voice to get people's attention. You've got a message to deliver, you're stoked to share it, and folks want to hear it! This is a great period for mingling, networking and posting important stories on social media. It's an extra-long

cycle because Mercury will be retrograde from October 31 to November 20. If things don't happen as fast as you'd like, be patient; they will soon enough!

October 3: Pluto retrograde ends

No more walking on eggshells! You may have felt like you had to watch your every move—and every word that came out of your mouth—with the controlling planet retrograde in your communication zone for the past five months. When it resumes forward motion today, it's safe to exhale!

October 4-November 19: Mars in Libra

Feeling low-energy? Don't just "soldier through" for the next six weeks. With your co-ruler, action planet Mars, slow-jamming through your restful twelfth house, the best thing you can do for yourself is pay attention to what your body is saying and honor its needs. If you know you've been burning the candle at both ends, extinguish it and take a break—make that *frequent* breaks.

October 7: Mercury-Uranus opposition

It's hard to know when to tell the truth, when to tell the whole truth, and if you should ever tell nothing *but* the truth. And it may be that you went a little too far in speaking your mind recently, and now you're trying to retract some of it. But with capricious Uranus in your dynamic-duos zone, you won't be able to read someone clearly. Rather than dig yourself in deeper, wait for them to make the next move.

October 7: Sun-Saturn square

It's easy to point the finger of blame when things aren't going your way, but a more mature (i.e., Saturn-approved) way of looking at the situation

would be to find *your* role in the situation. Under today's signal-jamming clash, the problem could be that you're thinking one thing yet saying something else—or saying what you mean but people are hearing something altogether different. Stop and clarify!

October 13: Aries full moon

Game on! The annual Aries full moon shines a spotlight on your organized, hardworking sixth house, giving you the motivational mojo to whip through your to-do list and clear the decks to start an inspiring new project. Where do you need help? Ask for it. (Or hire someone!)

October 14: Sun-Pluto square

The workweek begins with a bit of a poker game: Someone is trying to present themselves as honest and transparent, but you can practically see the ace up their sleeve! Yet in their "reality distortion field," you won't be able to call them on it. Busy yourself with your own work—and take nothing at face value.

October 15: Mercury-Neptune trine

The best way to get your message across today is with nonverbal communication. If you need to lead a meeting or make a presentation, use colorful and clear graphics and maybe some emotionally rousing music. Words will only be misconstrued, and you won't have the patience to reiterate.

October 27: Scorpio new moon

This golden lunation in your sign is like your cosmic New Year. This annual new moon in your sign can help you plant seeds for some of the things you're most excited to get off the ground. Over the coming two weeks, set aside quiet time to write down some inspirational goals, including a timeline of when you want to see them manifested.

October 27: Mars-Saturn square

Trust that little voice in your head or gut feeling that's telling you something is off. Is someone saying one thing and acting in a clearly contradictory way? Don't assume this will just resolve itself. It's more likely to blow up than blow over.

October 28: Sun-Uranus opposition

Be on the lookout for a frenemy—or out-and-out competitor—in sheep's clothing today. With the Sun (representing your ego and creativity) sliding into a shifty opposition with unpredictable Uranus in your house of alliances, someone might try to pull the wool over your eyes. But if you're ready for their shady moves, they won't stand a chance!

October 31-November 20: Mercury retrograde in Scorpio

The good news? This is the cosmic communicator's final retrograde of the year, so you won't have to field those wild mercurial pitches again until 2020! The downside? It's happening in your sign, so it might not just be your words and meaning that get scrambled…it could be any- and everything you try to put out in the world. This doesn't mean three weeks of hiding under the covers, though. Just take your time, be extra cautious, and hold off on big reveals, tech purchases or launches until the messenger planet comes correct.

NOVEMBER: LOVE HOTSPOTS

November 1-25: Venus in Sagittarius

You can strike a beautiful balance between excitement and stability when the love planet beams into adventurous Sagittarius and your second house of emotional security today. Having a reliable partner in and of itself is sexy; the physical attraction is the cherry on top. Looking for love? Focus on finding a person who shares these values—someone with a track record to prove it!

November 12: Taurus full moon

The annual Taurus full moon illuminates your seventh house of committed relationships, and in the sign of the steadfast Bull, you'll be more interested in being with someone who can actually go the distance! Be clear about your desires and let your partner know what you need. Single? Set the bar high and keep it there. Dedication to diverse dating efforts over the coming months will pay off!

November 14: Venus-Neptune square

Not everyone can fill all your needs at the same time, so keep your expectations realistic. With the love planet in your house of emotional security, you're playing for keeps. Yet today's clash with dreamweaver Neptune in your passionate fifth house could make you crave romantic fantasy. Weigh your options, and at least try to take the long view into consideration.

November 19-January 3: Mars in Scorpio

When your co-ruler, passionate Mars, returns to your sign for the first time in two years—and sticks around for six weeks—you may feel like you're making up for lost (or is that lust?) time. You won't have to work at turning up the heat: You'll be giving off sparks! And there's no reason to hold back. Go ahead, Scorpio: Let your spicy, seductive side out to play.

November 24: Venus-Jupiter meetup

This rare and auspicious planetary pairing is like a royal flush! It only happens once a year, and when the love planet and lucky Jupiter team up in spontaneous Sagittarius and your lush second house, something electrifying could happen in the blink of an eye. Celebrate your sizzling sensuality with a hot date.

November 24: Mars-Uranus opposition

Fools rush in…and out! With these two impulsive, hotheaded planets facing off, you could come on way too strong or race into a commitment before really knowing someone. Similarly, the impulse to rashly call things off could strike. Bottom line: Avoid any irreversible decisions in the days surrounding this impetuous showdown.

November 25-December 20: Venus in Capricorn

Loving Venus enters your communication house for a second time this year (it was here from February 3 to March 1). The holidays could feel like a bonus round of Valentine's Day, especially if you open up and tell people how you feel. Did Cupid miss the mark the first time? Witty banter under the mistletoe could remedy that, stat!

November 27: Neptune retrograde ends

At long last, clarity arrives. When the hazy planet straightens out after a five-month retrograde in

your romance sector, the fog lifts, confusion clears up and you can get your love life back on track once again.

November 28: Venus-Uranus trine

Look before you leap—into bed—especially if this involves a friend. Even if this erstwhile platonic pal is the most irresistible thing in sight, make sure you're not jeopardizing a valuable connection. For couples, an authentic conversation might be a little bit jarring, but the truth that gets revealed could strengthen your bond, and pave the way for more honest dialogue going forward.

NOVEMBER: CAREER HOTSPOTS

November 5: Mars-Pluto square

Your innocent or honest comment could bring the trolls out from under their bridges today, thanks to a clash between your celestial guardians. Of course these haters will try to push your buttons, but don't take the bait. Close your social media sites and get back to that important project you're working on!

November 8: Sun-Neptune trine

Let your creativity shine! With the bold Sun and imaginative Neptune in the most spotlight-grabbing parts of your chart, dare to share your most out-there ideas. You could attract more attention than you expected, so prepare to win a few new fans just by being your full-bodied self.

November 12: Taurus full moon

This once-a-year event in your dynamic-duos zone could light the path to a mutually advantageous partnership. In the sign of the grounded Bull, this lunar light reminds you that you can't take too many precautions, so get your terms in writing—and lawyer up if need be.

November 13: Mercury-Neptune trine

With the communication planet high-fiving Neptune, you might think you're being clear as a bell. But two things to consider: Mercury is retrograde (hello, scrambled signals), and Neptune always provides the fog. Since you may not realize that you're sending conflicting messages, sit down with the recipients and hash things out so everyone's definitely on the same page.

November 19-January 3: Mars in Scorpio

You're on fire! When motivator extraordinaire Mars marches into your sign, you'll have a dozen brilliant ideas that you're dying to get working on *now*! Since the red planet is better at starting things than finishing them, make sure to prioritize, set up timelines,and pace yourself.

November 20: Mercury retrograde ends

At last! Communicator Mercury ends a three-week retrograde backspin through *your* sign that started on October 31. If you've felt wildly misunderstood or had to deal with delays on a passion project, you'll start to see momentum again. Investing in technology or a new mode of transportation also gets easier with Mercury back on track.

November 24: Mars-Uranus opposition

People will be working your nerves today, but be careful about unloading on them, especially if you interact on a regular basis. You could burn an important bridge with a knee-jerk response. The urge to impulsively rush into a collaboration could also strike. Think twice before making anything official under these rash and reactive skies.

November 26: Sagittarius new moon

If you squint, you might see your ship coming in on the horizon! The year's only new moon in your money and work house lays a solid foundation for profitable developments over the next six months. But first you need to know what you want. Are you looking for a new gig—or a new career? Put the word out (discreetly) and see what leads come back to you. Or request a sit-down with your supervisor to see where you might grow within the company in the months to come.

November 28: Mercury-Neptune trine

Your thinking is more visionary than laser-sharp under this distorting mashup of mental Mercury and fuzzy Neptune. But that's okay: There's a time for spreadsheets and a time for ideation. Today is all about the latter!

DECEMBER: LOVE HOTSPOTS

December 11: Venus-Saturn meetup

This is the year's second and final Venus-Saturn mashup in your communication corner (the first was on February 18). If you had "the talk" back then but need a tune-up—or if you put it off altogether—now's the time! Single? Lead with your intellectual curiosity and wit and you'll have people eating out of your hand!

December 12: Gemini full moon

Draw the blinds, unplug the phones—but maybe turn on the A/C? Today marks the year's only full moon in your eighth house of intimacy and eroticism, and things could get mighty steamy behind closed doors. You may connect with strong feelings you weren't even aware existed. This lunation could bring a budding relationship to full bloom or, since full moons can also signal endings, it might mean a breakup is inevitable.

December 13: Mars-Neptune trine

Reality can be overrated! As your co-ruler, passionate Mars, in your sign embraces fantasy-fueled Neptune in your lusty fifth house, a slightly impractical romance may heat up—or you might just have the best first date ever! Relish the vibes, but keep your eyes open. If you've been trying to get pregnant, this is an especially fertile time.

December 13: Venus-Pluto meetup

Conversations could go from mild to wild in half a sentence under this hot-and-heavy mashup. And it's not necessarily superficial banter. If you mean what you're saying, dialogues today could prove to be nothing short of transformational.

December 20-January 13: Venus in Aquarius

When the amorous planet sets up camp in your sentimental fourth house, your nostalgic side may dominate. Just in time for the holidays, this annual spell of domestic bliss could inspire a key exchange, serious talks about moving in together or building a family. Break out the good linens and dishes—you may be very much in the mood to entertain!

December 22: Venus-Uranus square

Disruptive vibes prevail under this capricious clash. It may be "business as usual" for *you*, but someone might have their knickers in a knot for reasons you can't get a read on. Since they themselves might be clueless about what's driving this, cut them plenty of slack—at least, until tomorrow.

DECEMBER: CAREER HOTSPOTS

December 2, 2019-December 19, 2020: Jupiter in Capricorn

Even with the holidays upon you, it's time to up-level your work game and prepare for an expansive new chapter to begin! Auspicious Jupiter kicks off an exciting 13-month trek through your communication house, and people may seek you out for your ideas and ability to package them in a clear and persuasive way. In the coming weeks and months, reflect on what message you want to put out to the world. Since this realm also rules local happenings, you may become a player in your own virtual backyard.

December 8: Sun-Neptune square

Talk is cheap, and anyone can dream big. So if you want to actually pull off your grand plan, you're going to have to drill down deep and make sure all the nitty-gritty details will work. With idealistic Neptune confronting the Sun in your grounded second house, you'll meet with challenge if you don't have everything locked down.

December 9-28: Mercury in Sagittarius

Just in time to balance the books and close out 2019, analytical Mercury alights in your second house of finances. Not only can you get things in order but you can hatch some inspirational goals for the new year, with a heavy emphasis on increasing your bottom line. You already have some ideas, from forging a new strategic partnership to cutting costs.

December 12: Gemini full moon

Team up to level up! The year's only full moon in your house of joint ventures and investments can motivate you to find the perfect partner to help you launch a project you've been sitting on. Before 2019 ends, sit down (preferably with a financial planner) to make sure your funds are properly allocated. No adviser? Finding a good one might be your next priority!

December 15: Jupiter-Uranus trine

You may insist you're not a "group" person, Scorpio, but as effusive Jupiter and innovative Uranus meld their superpowers in your relationship houses, you could meet a kindred spirit when you least expect it. This is an extremely rare meetup of these adventurous planets, so a person who crosses your path today could become hugely important. Conversations might also lead to life-changing ideas. Don't dismiss the dynamic-duo potential or a serendipitous encounter. Tuck your phone away and be present—a little eye contact may turn into much more.

December 19: Mercury-Neptune square

Mind your budget! As holiday shopping season pressure bears down, you might be tempted to make some rash (read: overpriced) purchases, but there's no need for that. First, focus on nailing a deadline; then, when you're free and clear, devote a few hours to your gift list. If you don't succumb

to stress, you'll remember that you're in the driver's seat here.

December 24: Sun-Uranus trine

Your brain doesn't realize it's Christmas Eve, so if the most brilliant idea you've had all month just happens to strike today, get it down on paper or into your notes app and give it three asterisks. Even if you can't do anything about this for another week, you can tumble it in your head and polish it until it comes out a perfect gem!

December 26: Capricorn new moon (solar eclipse)

The second Capricorn new moon of the year is also an *annular* solar eclipse (also called a "ring of fire"), and as it falls in your ideas sector, it could spark some big ideas! Pay extra attention to "casual" conversations in the next two weeks. Contained within them could be the seeds for a profitable collaboration that unfolds slowly but steadily (i.e., Capricorn-style) over the coming six months.

December 27: Sun-Jupiter meetup

This might just be the luckiest day of the year, as the life-affirming Sun and propitious Jupiter team up in your mental sector. You're feeling sharp, inspired and on-point today, so reach out to someone you've been trying to pitch—or just post your message online to reach the widest possible audience. You never know where this will lead until you try.

December 28-January 16: Mercury in Capricorn

When the mentally nimble planet sprints through your expressive third house for the next three weeks, you've got the talking stick. This is a perfect time to explore creative synergies with potential collaborators. While you mostly want to listen, a good way to get the other parties to open up is to ask a lot of smart and sincere questions.

December 30: Mercury-Uranus trine

Intriguing collaborations could ignite with witty Mercury and innovative Uranus aligned in your interpersonal houses. Sure, it's almost the end of the year and everyone's presumably offline, but see what happens when you publish a compelling post on social media or a thoughtful blog about, say, how we all need to work together in the new decade. Parties and events could turn up fabulous connections, so don't even think about hiding out at home tomorrow night! ✳

82

2019 NUMEROLOGY

3

THE 3 UNIVERSAL YEAR

By Felicia Bender

THE PRACTICAL NUMEROLOGIST

THE 3 UNIVERSAL YEAR

Make connections! A year of creativity and self-expression awaits.

In numerology, each calendar year adds up to a single-digit number, which resonates at a unique vibration. We all feel this energy, and it's called the Universal Year.

A Universal Year means that everyone on the planet will experience the frequency of a particular number during the entire year, from January 1 until December 31.

Whether or not you make New Year's resolutions, most of us intuitively feel a profound energy shift whenever the calendar turns. In numerology, that transition is a big deal, marking the passage into a new Universal Year—the shared atmosphere of the world for a 12-month period.

You can think of the Universal Year as the state or country you're driving through on your yearly "road trip." The Universal Year number will set the GPS and chart our collective course.

Where We're Coming From

The progression of Universal Years from 1 to 9 is a complete journey, so we look at the surrounding years to see where we're coming from and where we're headed. In 2017, which was a 1 Universal Year, we began a whole new cycle—and the world certainly reflected that.

Next, 2018 was a Master 11/2 Universal Year. Master numbers are repeating numbers like 11, 22 and 33, which create a secondary vibration, giving the year an infusion of paradox and power. These numbers carry a higher frequency and demand evolution.

Last year's Universal energy brought a higher spiritual purpose to the planet, and also ramped up the intensity. We were pulled between the

How to Calculate the Universal Year:

Add the individual numbers of the current year together, like this:

2019 = 2 + 0 + 1 + 9 = 12

Then reduce again:

1 + 2 = 3

2019 is a 3 Universal Year

All of us will begin to feel this energy starting January 1, 2019 and the effect will end on December 31, 2019.

cooperation, or at least with mutual respect. However successful we were with that mission, either globally *or* locally, it became clear that we had to rise above the divisiveness that's been destroying our world.

While the energy and events of 2018 are still impacting us, a shift in perspective is coming our way. 2019 offers up a reconfiguration of our core sense of reality and our place within it. That's no small feat. And that change won't happen overnight or in one 12-month cycle of time. In fact, each time a Universal Year rings in, it begins a whole new cycle until that same Universal Year number returns a decade later.

The 3 Universal Year

The number 3 in numerology is the vibration of creative self-expression and emotional sensitivity. It emanates joy, optimism, social engagement and communication. Universally, we're being offered energy that supports infusing creativity, fun and connection into all that we do. Humor and lightness hold immense power and can help us face any heaviness or monumental change.

This year will help us take the spiritual illumination initiated by 2018 and infuse it into a newfound sense of purpose and power.

The most enlightened use of the number 3 is to inspire and uplift others. This Universal Year is set up as a blank canvas awaiting our most meaningful contributions. The mantra for the 3 Universal Year is to *speak your truth*. But in order to do so, you have

diplomatic "2" energy of love, patience, and cooperation, while also navigating a double dose of the contrasting "1" energy, which emphasizes individuality, taking initiative and flying solo.

As a result, it was a year of oppositions that heightened feeling of division and polarity: us/them, love/hate, war/peace material/spiritual. While that was tough to navigate, the more "enlightened" mission was to discover our collective responsibility—to ourselves and each other.

The balancing beams of the 11/2 Universal Year called on us to start working in harmonious

The AstroTwins' 2019 Planetary Planner

to know what your "truth" even is—and (hint) it's not just an uninformed opinion or knee-jerk reaction to the latest headlines.

And that's where it gets tricky: How do we hold on to our own truth while allowing others to have theirs? How do we express our beliefs and stand up for ourselves when our values don't align with someone else's? How do we discern the difference between "truth" and "values"? Or "truth" and "integrity"? Or "truth" and "dogma"?

Author Byron Katie, who teaches a self-inquiry method called The Work, suggests that beliefs are just thoughts we think over and over again. When we change our thoughts, we change our beliefs. Katie's method involves asking yourself these four questions, especially if something that's become a fixed belief, or "truth," in your head is causing you to suffer:

Is it true?

Can you absolutely know it's true?

How do you react—what happens—when you believe that thought?

Who would you be without this thought?

It seems the first step in this 3 Universal Year is to reflect on what we've adopted as the truth before speaking, typing or posting a word. The seemingly simple act of "speaking your truth" turns out not to be so simple after all. It's a layered process, and one we'll all be supported in exploring in 2019: Connecting with our individual, and then collective, truth—and expressing it in a healthy, respectful and transformative way.

3 is the number of creation and this is an extremely fertile year for all forms of creativity. In addition to novel problem-solving, scientific and medical innovation, and new environmental solutions, the 3 Universal Year highlights the arts as a conduit for expression on all levels. We have seen how artistic communities have stepped forward and used their influence to speak out about everything from global warming to saying, "Time's Up!" to sexual predators and gender discrimination. This influence will gain even more velocity and power in 2019.

How to Step into The Creative Power of the 3 Universal Year
Practice impeccable communication.

The energy of the year demands that we brush up on our communication skills across the board. This holds true for our most intimate relationships, extends to the way we express ourselves at work, and bleeds over into all our engagements, large and small. How do you speak to yourself? What's your internal dialogue? Is it true, kind and constructive? How do you speak to your friends and family? Are you able to "be yourself" no matter what your surroundings? How do you speak to the person working the drive-through or to the barista who makes your coffee? This is a time to truly choose your words with mindful precision. When in doubt, listen twice as much as you speak.

Lighten up and see new possibilities.

The gift of the number 3 is its bright light of fun, wit and humor. Think about it: Do we learn the most when the task is serious and punishing? Or do we absorb more when the lesson feels like play   when we laugh along the way, and feel supported and validated as we make mistakes *and* as we succeed?

Intelligent and curious, the 3 thrives when delving into the depths of expression, spinning the old into something novel and fresh. Before you throw out the baby with the bathwater, see if you can salvage or reinvent a situation. The best use of a 3 Universal Year is to take existing ideas and concepts and "upcycle" them. Create new twists on services and products to make them into something fresh and relevant that serves the greater good. The 3 Universal Year opens us up to new ideas, and challenges us to also inspire others along the way.

Learn something new.

2019 is the year to "upgrade thyself." No more driving in the same ruts in the road. Mentally, physically and spiritually, the 3 Universal Year encourages us to go boldly into new and improved terrain. Treat life like an adventure! The magic manifests when we infuse a sense of joy and optimism into everything we do. This will build on the independence and individuality we've gained over the last two Universal Years. Take the independence of the 1 Year (and last year's

Master number 11), grab a buddy as a nod to the 2 Year's cooperative vibe, and head off on that unchartered mission. You'll thrive when you give new experiences a go!

Challenges of the 3 Universal Year
Manage your emotions.

One of the issues with the energy of the number 3 is that it brings *all* of our emotions to the table—the good, the bad and the ugly—not to mention the known, unknown and repressed. The 3 Universal Year demands that we get real and responsible about our feelings. The year will be full of global trigger points, and it will demand higher levels of self-awareness so that we're not all walking around raging and reacting to everything that pushes our buttons.

As the saying goes, feelings are not facts. But for some people, the energy of the 3 will bring choppy emotional waves that can translate into depressive or melancholy moments. It would be a good time to revisit Eckhardt Tolle's *The Power of Now,* which teaches us how to become observers of our thoughts and feelings, rather than getting caught up in their maelstrom. That may require being vigilant about the conversations we have and the thoughts we simply accept at face value, ones that trigger a whole cascade of brain chemicals and reactions.

The film *What the Bleep Do We Know?* gives a fascinating look at the neuroscience behind our emotional reactions. Well worth watching!

       The AstroTwins' 2019 Planetary Planner

Stick it out—you've got this!

As buoyant as 3 energy can be, it can also provoke severe moments of self-doubt that cause us to waver in our commitments. The 3 can be scattered—and this year, we may find ourselves starting lots of projects and losing steam before we finish. Watch out for a distracting case of Shiny Object Syndrome. During a 3 Universal Year we can all benefit from gentle focus and active follow-through. Consider putting a "Pomodoro timer" app on your smartphone to help you work in focused bursts or teaming up with an accountability partner to help you stay on track.

Think before you speak.

It'll be a challenge to not only watch our words (while speaking "authentically,"), but also to bring precision to the way we communicate. That means: Choosing the proper words. Choosing not to gossip or tear others apart with sarcasm and hurtful snipes. Choosing to get more in touch with our truth—and to speak it with consistency and grace.

The Big Picture

Overall, the 3 Universal Year shines a spotlight on creative self-expression, joy, optimism and authentic communication. The year brings opportunities to express new ideas and discover novel approaches to broken systems. It's earmarked for all of us to take an honest look at how we express our feelings, desires and fears.

Despite deep unrest we feel on a global scale, the universal energy for 2019 invites us into the sandbox, onto the stage and into the spotlight. It reminds us to play and laugh, to find lightness in the shadows and to shine our light into the dark crevices in order to bring creative solutions to the planet. ✳

Felicia Bender, Ph.D. (The Practical Numerologist) is Astrostyle's resident numerologist and author of *Redesign Your Life: Using Numerology to Create the Wildly Optimal You* and *Master Numbers 11, 22, and 33: The Ultimate Guide.* Follow her at www.FeliciaBender.com.

2019
CHINESE HOROSCOPE

YEAR OF THE EARTH PIG

YEAR OF THE EARTH PIG

In Chinese astrology, the pleasure-loving, sociable Earth Pig will reign from February 5, 2019, until January 25, 2020.

Come on out of the doghouse—there's a party in the pen! As we celebrate the Chinese (Lunar) New Year this February 5, 2019, the Year of the Earth Pig begins, kicking off the night before with the Lunar New Year's Eve on February 4. After two intense years, this convivial cycle gives us a chance to "rest and digest." The pregnant pause of 2019 might even help us make some sense of all the global mudslinging that's been going around. Serenity now?

The pleasant and genial Earth Pig's arrival will be a welcome relief after 2018's Earth Dog antics. Dogs are pack animals, and in the past year, groups have stuck together out of "loyalty," at times, to a fault. It's widely agreed that the world has never felt more divided, and no surprise that the coop-stalking energy of 2017's Rooster and the border-guarding vibes of 2018's Dog spiraled into xenophobic extremes. To wit, hate crimes have increased internationally and last year saw the tragic separation of children from parents who were seeking asylum at the U.S. border.

Reinstate that open-door policy! The Earth Pig's M.O. is far more welcoming. This friendly creature can be quite the social butterfly, with pals from all walks of life. In 2019, a good bottle of vino—not a good fence—makes a good neighbor. (From #WineTime to #SwineTime?)

Pigs are complex communicators who dream, recognize their own names and have over twenty oinks and squeaks that have been identified with an actual language that they share. Some scientists believe that their social skills rival those of primates. Unlike the territorial animals who governed 2017 and 2018, Rooster and Dog, the easygoing Pig cohabitates well with other barnyard species. Perhaps 2019 will be the year where people start engaging in legitimate dialogues again, instead of simply barking at each through the "picture window" of social media.

During the Earth Dog's tenure in 2018, our homes were our shelters. Many people spent a pretty penny on décor and tucked away in their comfy nests. But what's the fun of splurging on the hand-loomed textiles and thrown-ceramic dishes if you can't show them off to guests? Cocktail parties will be de rigueur again in 2019, with a rainbow coalition of guests in attendance. We might even resume "dressing for dinner," instead of rocking the athleisure at five-star venues.

Forget what you heard about a messy room being a "pigsty" or people "sweating like pigs." While real-world swines roll around in mud to cool off, they are clean creatures by nature. In the year ahead, our spaces may become a lot more orderly and neat. No leaving dishes stacked up by the sink for days

90

after those soirees—or indulging in excess plastic packaging that winds up floating in the oceans and being digested by fish. (Scary!) Cleanliness is next to godliness during the Earth Pig year. That said, Pigs are known for having their lazy spells. This might be the year to hire a housekeeper for a regular deep clean, especially if you're the type who "doesn't do windows."

Who do you call a friend? Alas, the Earth Pig isn't always the most discerning creature. In 2019, guilt by association can be an issue for folks who naively get caught up with the wrong crowd. Mingling at the pub and exchanging pleasantries with friendly acquaintances? That's one thing. But before declaring anyone "squad," make sure you know their true background. Are they playing dirty behind the scenes? Appearances can be deceiving during the Year of the Earth Pig. Bottom line: Don't let other people wipe their mud on your clean reputation and sully your name.

When it comes to love, the Earth Pig isn't exactly the most romantic creature. In 2019, we may have to work a little harder to cultivate the sexy sparks. That said, the Pig is associated with Scorpio in the Western zodiac, and it's certainly possible to bring out our "wild boars" in the bedroom. (Easy with those tusks, please.) Like Scorpio, the Pig is a water sign in the Chinese zodiac—capable of deep and powerful emotion. And yet, the intensity of those feelings might be a bit much for people to bear,

What's Your Chinese Zodiac Sign?

Rat: 1924, 1936, 1948, 1960, 1972, 1984, 1996, 2008
Ox: 1925, 1937, 1949, 1961, 1973, 1985, 1997, 2009
Tiger: 1926, 1938, 1950, 1962, 1974, 1986, 1998, 2010
Rabbit: 1927, 1939, 1951, 1963, 1975, 1987, 1999, 2011
Dragon: 1928, 1940, 1952, 1964, 1976, 1988, 2000, 2012
Snake: 1929, 1941, 1953, 1965, 1977, 1989, 2001, 2013
Horse: 1930, 1942, 1954, 1966, 1978, 1990, 2002, 2014
Sheep: 1931, 1943, 1955, 1967, 1979, 1991, 2003, 2015
Monkey: 1932, 1944, 1956, 1968, 1980, 1992, 2004, 2016
Rooster: 1933, 1945, 1957, 1969, 1981, 1993, 2005, 2017
Dog: 1934, 1946, 1958, 1970, 1982, 1994, 2006, 2019
Pig: 1935, 1947, 1959, 1971, 1983, 1995, 2007, 2019

especially with the grounded Earth energy ruling this year. No need to process every trauma all at once in 2019; just deal in small and therapeutic kilobytes. And don't forget that fun and laughter can be anti-depressants, too.

The last time we had an Earth Pig year was 1959. On the surface, it was an uneventful period in history—despite Fidel Castro coming into power on February 16, the grand finale to 1958's Alpha-empowering Earth Dog cycle. But a few key developments emerged under the Earth Pig's tenure. The microchip was invented, which is the foundation of the Digital Age in which we now live. Research officially began on the birth-control pill and Alaska and Hawaii became the 49th and 50th states—a nod to the Earth Pig's inclusive diplomacy. The Barbie doll was introduced to the world in 1959, an unwitting symbol of the "plastic is fantastic" superficiality that can mark an Earth Pig year. And, the ribbon was cut on the visually arresting Guggenheim Museum in New York City, which houses many modern and "eccentric" works of art.

Interestingly, on July 24, 1959, then-Vice President Richard Nixon got swept into the famous "kitchen debate" with Soviet Premier Nikita Khrushchev. During an exhibition that was meant to foster cultural exchange between the U.S. and Russia, the gloves came off as the two leaders began a verbal battle about capitalism versus communism.

The finger-pointing drama took place in a model kitchen that was set up as part of the exhibit as Nixon suggested that Khrushchev's threats of using nuclear power could lead to war. In the end—and in true Earth Pig style—both leaders pulled back from the debate and claimed a desire for peace. With U.S. and Russian relations see-sawing wildly after proven election hacking and unprecedented summits, it will be interesting to see what this Earth Pig year brings.

Health-wise, Earth Pig years are times where we might have to monitor our diets more carefully. It's easy to overdo it on the sweets and rich foods. (And watch that "liquid courage"!) Gentler forms of exercise like hiking and swimming are favored—and sleep sanctity should be honored in the name of keeping our immune systems strong.

Financially, the Earth Pig is slowly, but steadily, abundant. This zodiac sign has a solid work ethic and is willing to put in the hours to get ahead. Patience and willpower are the name of the game for anyone wishing to get ahead in 2019. And don't forget the power of building friendly alliances with colleagues. Pigs are often the office optimists and motivators; the ones who will keep the team spirit burning bright.

Want to mark yourself as a rising star? In addition to delivering solid work in 2019, be the "crew glue" of your coworkers, rallying everyone for a company picnic or happy hour and keeping the momentum

> **"Financially, the Earth Pig has a solid work ethic and is willing to put in the long hours to get ahead."**

strong. Where Pigs can fall short is in setting clear-cut goals and a solid schedule. Work harder to implement those project management systems and you'll be sure to succeed in 2019.

On a global level, employment will be a hot topic of discussion. Creating (and retaining) jobs will be an important mission for many countries, which may require some fancy economic footwork. Since people will be out and about more often, 2019 could bring a boon for the hospitality, fashion and entertainment industries. While the Earth Pig certainly doesn't mind a powerful title, this is not necessarily a super-ambitious year. Quality of life is as important as a paycheck and some people may decide that a slower pace is more fulfilling than endlessly climbing the corporate ladder.

Money management may be a struggle in 2019. The indulgent Earth Pig loves fine food, vintage bubbles and elegant fashion house finds. Under this feel-good spell, there will be days when we might just want to buy a round of champagne for an entire bar of strangers. Fun, fun, fun...but what about the funds? In 2019, we'll have to be careful not to burn as fast as we earn.

To avoid such slips, it would be wise to create a set-and-forget financial plan. Activate the auto-pay features for your monthly utilities or have money transferred into savings and investment accounts. If you don't see it, you won't spend it. Just make sure you also create an entertainment fund!

2019
COSMIC
CALENDAR

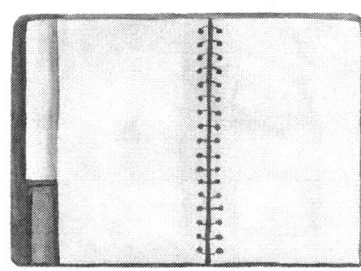

DAILY
PLANETARY GUIDE

January 2019

MONDAY

1   TUESDAY

2   WEDNESDAY

3   THURSDAY

4 ☿ Mercury enters Capricorn   FRIDAY

5 ♑ Capricorn new moon (partial solar eclipse) ●   SATURDAY

6 ♅ Uranus retrograde in Aries   SUNDAY

The AstroTwins' 2019 Planetary Planner   96

January 2019

7 ♀ Venus enters Sagittarius — MONDAY

8 — TUESDAY

9 — WEDNESDAY

10 — THURSDAY

11 — FRIDAY

12 — SATURDAY

13 Waxing quarter moon in Aries ☽ — SUNDAY

The AstroTwins' 2019 Planetary Planner

January 2019

| 14 | MONDAY |

| 15 | TUESDAY |

| 16 | WEDNESDAY |

| 17 | THURSDAY |

| 18 | FRIDAY |

| 19 | SATURDAY |

| 20 | ♒ Sun enters Aquarius | SUNDAY |

January 2019

21   ♌ Leo full moon (total lunar eclipse & supermoon) ○   MONDAY

22   TUESDAY

23   WEDNESDAY

24   ☿ Mercury enters Aquarius   THURSDAY

25   FRIDAY

26   SATURDAY

27   Waning quarter moon in Scorpio ◑   SUNDAY

The AstroTwins' 2019 Planetary Planner

January 2019

28	MONDAY
29	TUESDAY
30	WEDNESDAY
31	THURSDAY
	FRIDAY
	SATURDAY
	SUNDAY

100

February 2019

MONDAY

TUESDAY

WEDNESDAY

THURSDAY

1   FRIDAY

2   SATURDAY

3 ♀ Venus enters Capricorn   SUNDAY

February 2019

4 ♒ Aquarius new moon ●   MONDAY

5 Chinese New Year (Earth Pig)   TUESDAY

6   WEDNESDAY

7   THURSDAY

8   FRIDAY

9   SATURDAY

10 ☿ Mercury enters Pisces   SUNDAY

The AstroTwins' 2019 Planetary Planner   102

February 2019

11 —— MONDAY

12 Waxing quarter moon in Taurus ☽ ———————————— TUESDAY

13 —— WEDNESDAY

14 ♂ Mars enters Taurus ——————————————————————— THURSDAY

15 —— FRIDAY

16 —— SATURDAY

17 —— SUNDAY

         The AstroTwins' 2019 Planetary Planner

February 2019

18 ♓ Sun enters Pisces — MONDAY

19 ♍ Virgo full moon (supermoon) ○ — TUESDAY

20 — WEDNESDAY

21 — THURSDAY

22 — FRIDAY

23 — SATURDAY

24 — SUNDAY

February 2019

25 ── MONDAY

26 ── TUESDAY
Waning quarter moon in Sagittarius ◑

27 ── WEDNESDAY

28 ── THURSDAY

── FRIDAY

── SATURDAY

── SUNDAY

March 2019

	MONDAY

	TUESDAY

	WEDNESDAY

	THURSDAY

1 ♀ Venus enters Aquarius — FRIDAY

2 — SATURDAY

3 — SUNDAY

The AstroTwins' 2019 Planetary Planner   106

March 2019

4   MONDAY

5 ☿ Mercury retrograde in Pisces   TUESDAY

6 ♓ Pisces new moon ●   WEDNESDAY
    ♅ Uranus enters Taurus

7   THURSDAY

8   FRIDAY

9   SATURDAY

10   SUNDAY

The AstroTwins' 2019 Planetary Planner

March 2019

11	MONDAY
12	TUESDAY
13	WEDNESDAY
14 Waxing quarter moon in Gemini ◑	THURSDAY
15	FRIDAY
16	SATURDAY
17	SUNDAY

March 2019

| 18 | MONDAY |

| 19 | TUESDAY |

| 20 | ♈ Sun enters Aries | WEDNESDAY |
| | ♎ Libra full moon | |

| 21 | THURSDAY |

| 22 | FRIDAY |

| 23 | SATURDAY |

| 24 | SUNDAY |

The AstroTwins' 2019 Planetary Planner

March 2019

25	MONDAY

26	♀ Venus enters Pisces	TUESDAY

27	WEDNESDAY

28	☿ Mercury retrograde ends	THURSDAY

Waning quarter moon in Capricorn ◑

29	FRIDAY

30	SATURDAY

31	♂ Mars enters Gemini	SUNDAY

April 2019

1   MONDAY

2   TUESDAY

3   WEDNESDAY

4   THURSDAY

5   ♈ Aries new moon ●   FRIDAY

6   SATURDAY

7   SUNDAY

April 2019

8		MONDAY

9		TUESDAY

10	♃ Jupiter retrograde in Sagittarius	WEDNESDAY

11		THURSDAY

12	Waxing quarter moon in Cancer ◑	FRIDAY

13		SATURDAY

14		SUNDAY

April 2019

15   MONDAY

16   TUESDAY

17 ☿ Mercury enters Aries   WEDNESDAY

18   THURSDAY

19 ♎ Libra full moon ○   FRIDAY

20 ♉ Sun enters Taurus   SATURDAY
    ♀ Venus enters Aries

21   SUNDAY

              The AstroTwins' 2019 Planetary Planner

April 2019

22	MONDAY
23	TUESDAY
24 ♇ Pluto retrograde in Capricorn	WEDNESDAY
25	THURSDAY
26 Waning quarter moon in Aquarius ◑	FRIDAY
27	SATURDAY
28	SUNDAY

The AstroTwins' 2019 Planetary Planner — 114 —

April 2019

29 ♄ Saturn retrograde in Capricorn   MONDAY

30   TUESDAY

WEDNESDAY

THURSDAY

FRIDAY

SATURDAY

SUNDAY

        115

May 2019

MONDAY

TUESDAY

1   WEDNESDAY

2   THURSDAY

3   FRIDAY

4   ♉ Taurus new moon ●   SATURDAY

5   SUNDAY

May 2019

6	☿ Mercury enters Taurus	MONDAY
7		TUESDAY
8		WEDNESDAY
9		THURSDAY
10		FRIDAY
11	Waxing quarter moon in Leo ☽	SATURDAY
12		SUNDAY

The AstroTwins' 2019 Planetary Planner

May 2019

13 ———————————————————————— MONDAY

14 ———————————————————————— TUESDAY

15 ———————————————————————— WEDNESDAY
♀ Venus enters Taurus
♂ Mars enters Cancer

16 ———————————————————————— THURSDAY

17 ———————————————————————— FRIDAY

18 ———————————————————————— SATURDAY
♏ Scorpio full moon ○

19 ———————————————————————— SUNDAY

May 2019

20 _____ MONDAY

21 ♊ Sun enters Gemini _____ TUESDAY
☿ Mercury enters Gemini

22 _____ WEDNESDAY

23 _____ THURSDAY

24 _____ FRIDAY

25 _____ SATURDAY

26 Waning quarter moon in Pisces ◑ _____ SUNDAY

May 2019

27 ——————————————————————————————— MONDAY

28 ——————————————————————————————— TUESDAY

29 ——————————————————————————————— WEDNESDAY

30 ——————————————————————————————— THURSDAY

31 ——————————————————————————————— FRIDAY

——————————————————————————————— SATURDAY

——————————————————————————————— SUNDAY

The AstroTwins' 2019 Planetary Planner   120

June 2019

MONDAY

TUESDAY

WEDNESDAY

THURSDAY

FRIDAY

1

SATURDAY

2

SUNDAY

The AstroTwins' 2019 Planetary Planner

June 2019

3 ♊ Gemini new moon ●   MONDAY

4 ☿ Mercury enters Cancer   TUESDAY

5   WEDNESDAY

6   THURSDAY

7   FRIDAY

8 ♀ Venus enters Gemini   SATURDAY

9   SUNDAY

June 2019

10   Waxing quarter moon in Virgo ◑   MONDAY

11   TUESDAY

12   WEDNESDAY

13   THURSDAY

14   FRIDAY

15   SATURDAY

16   SUNDAY

The AstroTwins' 2019 Planetary Planner

June 2019

17 ♐ Sagittarius full moon — MONDAY

18 — TUESDAY

19 — WEDNESDAY

20 — THURSDAY

21 ♋ Sun enters Cancer — FRIDAY
♆ Neptune retrograde in Pisces

22 — SATURDAY

23 — SUNDAY

June 2019

24   MONDAY

25   Waning quarter moon in Aries ◑   TUESDAY

26   ☿ Mercury enters Leo   WEDNESDAY

27   THURSDAY

28   FRIDAY

29   SATURDAY

30   SUNDAY

 The AstroTwins' 2019 Planetary Planner

July 2019

1 ♂ Mars enters Leo — MONDAY

2 ♋ Cancer new moon (total solar eclipse) ● — TUESDAY

3 ♀ Venus enters Cancer — WEDNESDAY

4 — THURSDAY

5 — FRIDAY

6 — SATURDAY

7 ☿ Mercury retrograde in Leo — SUNDAY

July 2019

8   MONDAY

9   Waxing quarter moon in Libra ◑   TUESDAY

10   WEDNESDAY

11   THURSDAY

12   FRIDAY

13   SATURDAY

14   SUNDAY

        The AstroTwins' 2019 Planetary Planner

July 2019

15 — MONDAY

16 — ♑ Capricorn full moon (partial lunar eclipse) ○ — TUESDAY

17 — WEDNESDAY

18 — THURSDAY

19 — ☿ Mercury Rx enters Cancer — FRIDAY

20 — SATURDAY

21 — SUNDAY

July 2019

22 ♌ Sun enters Leo MONDAY

23   TUESDAY

24 Waning quarter moon in Taurus ◑ WEDNESDAY

25   THURSDAY

26   FRIDAY

27 ♀ Venus enters Leo SATURDAY

28   SUNDAY

    The AstroTwins' 2019 Planetary Planner

July 2019

29 — MONDAY

30 — TUESDAY

31 ♌ Leo new moon ● — WEDNESDAY
☿ Mercury retrograde ends

— THURSDAY

— FRIDAY

— SATURDAY

— SUNDAY

August 2019

MONDAY

TUESDAY

WEDNESDAY

1   THURSDAY

2   FRIDAY

3   SATURDAY

4   SUNDAY

The AstroTwins' 2019 Planetary Planner

August 2019

5   MONDAY

6   TUESDAY

7   Waxing quarter moon in Scorpio ◑   WEDNESDAY

8   THURSDAY

9   FRIDAY

10   SATURDAY

11   ☿ Mercury enters Leo   SUNDAY
     ♃ Jupiter retrograde ends
     ♅ Uranus retrograde in Taurus

August 2019

12 ——————————————————————————————— MONDAY

13 ——————————————————————————————— TUESDAY

14 ——————————————————————————————— WEDNESDAY

15 ♒︎ Aquarius full moon ○ ————————————— THURSDAY

16 ——————————————————————————————— FRIDAY

17 ——————————————————————————————— SATURDAY

18 ♂ Mars enters Virgo ————————————————— SUNDAY

The AstroTwins' 2019 Planetary Planner

August 2019

19	MONDAY

20	TUESDAY

21	WEDNESDAY

♀ Venus enters Virgo

22	THURSDAY

23	FRIDAY

♍ Sun in Virgo

Waning quarter moon in Gemini ◑

24	SATURDAY

25	SUNDAY

August 2019

26 _____ MONDAY

27 _____ TUESDAY

28 _____ WEDNESDAY

29 ☿ Mercury enters Virgo _____ THURSDAY

30 ♍ Virgo new moon ● _____ FRIDAY

31 _____ SATURDAY

_____ SUNDAY

 The AstroTwins' 2019 Planetary Planner

September 2019

MONDAY

TUESDAY

WEDNESDAY

THURSDAY

FRIDAY

SATURDAY

1

SUNDAY

September 2019

2 _____ MONDAY

3 _____ TUESDAY

4 _____ WEDNESDAY

5 Waxing quarter moon in Sagittarius ◐ THURSDAY

6 _____ FRIDAY

7 _____ SATURDAY

8 _____ SUNDAY

 The AstroTwins' 2019 Planetary Planner

September 2019

9	MONDAY

10	TUESDAY

11	WEDNESDAY

12	THURSDAY

13	FRIDAY

14
♓ Pisces full moon ○
☿ Mercury enters Libra
♀ Venus enters Libra

SATURDAY

15	SUNDAY

September 2019

16 _____ MONDAY

17 _____ TUESDAY

18 ♄ Saturn retrograde ends _____ WEDNESDAY

19 _____ THURSDAY

20 _____ FRIDAY

21 Waning quarter moon in Gemini ◑ _____ SATURDAY

22 _____ SUNDAY

 The AstroTwins' 2019 Planetary Planner

September 2019

23 ♎ Sun enters Libra   MONDAY

24   TUESDAY

25   WEDNESDAY

26   THURSDAY

27   FRIDAY

28 ♎ Libra new moon ●   SATURDAY

29   SUNDAY

September 2019

30
                                                      MONDAY

TUESDAY

WEDNESDAY

THURSDAY

FRIDAY

SATURDAY

SUNDAY

The AstroTwins' 2019 Planetary Planner

October 2019

1   MONDAY

2   TUESDAY

3   ☿ Mercury enters Scorpio   WEDNESDAY
     ♇ Pluto retrograde ends

4   ♂ Mars enters Libra   THURSDAY

5 Waxing quarter moon in Capricorn ◑   FRIDAY

6   SATURDAY

                                                SUNDAY

October 2019

7   MONDAY

8   ♀ Venus enters Scorpio   TUESDAY

9   WEDNESDAY

10   THURSDAY

11   FRIDAY

12   SATURDAY

13 ♈ Aries full moon ○   SUNDAY

                  The AstroTwins' 2019 Planetary Planner

October 2019

14   MONDAY

15   TUESDAY

16   WEDNESDAY

17   THURSDAY

18   FRIDAY

19   SATURDAY

20   SUNDAY

October 2019

21 Waning quarter moon in Cancer ◐   MONDAY

22   TUESDAY

23 ♏ Sun enters Scorpio   WEDNESDAY

24   THURSDAY

25   FRIDAY

26   SATURDAY

27 ♏ Scorpio new moon ●   SUNDAY

        The AstroTwins' 2019 Planetary Planner

October 2019

28 ——————————————————————— MONDAY

29 ——————————————————————— TUESDAY

30 ——————————————————————— WEDNESDAY

31 ☿ Mercury retrograde in Scorpio ——————— THURSDAY

——————————————————————————— FRIDAY

——————————————————————————— SATURDAY

——————————————————————————— SUNDAY

November 2019

MONDAY

TUESDAY

WEDNESDAY

THURSDAY

1 ♀ Venus enters Sagittarius

FRIDAY

2

SATURDAY

3

SUNDAY

November 2019

4 Waxing quarter moon in Aquarius ◑   MONDAY

5   TUESDAY

6   WEDNESDAY

7 Waxing quarter moon in Gemini ◑   THURSDAY

8   FRIDAY

9   SATURDAY

10   SUNDAY

November 2019

11	MONDAY
12 ♉ Taurus full moon ○	TUESDAY
13	WEDNESDAY
14	THURSDAY
15	FRIDAY
16	SATURDAY
17	SUNDAY

         The AstroTwins' 2019 Planetary Planner

November 2019

18 ———————————————————————————————— MONDAY

19 ♂ Mars enters Scorpio — TUESDAY
Waning quarter moon in Leo ☽

20 ☿ Mercury retrograde ends — WEDNESDAY

21 ———————————————————————————————— THURSDAY

22 ♐ Sun enters Sagittarius — FRIDAY

23 ———————————————————————————————— SATURDAY

24 ———————————————————————————————— SUNDAY

November 2019

25 ♀ Venus enters Capricorn — MONDAY

26 ♐ Sagittarius new moon ● — TUESDAY

27 ♆ Neptune retrograde ends — WEDNESDAY

28 — THURSDAY

29 — FRIDAY

30 — SATURDAY

SUNDAY

 The AstroTwins' 2019 Planetary Planner

December 2019

MONDAY

TUESDAY

WEDNESDAY

THURSDAY

FRIDAY

SATURDAY

1

SUNDAY

December 2019

2 ♃ Jupiter enters Capricorn — MONDAY

3 — TUESDAY

4 Waxing quarter moon in Pisces ◑ — WEDNESDAY

5 — THURSDAY

6 — FRIDAY

7 — SATURDAY

8 — SUNDAY

The AstroTwins' 2019 Planetary Planner

December 2019

9 ☿ Mercury enters Sagittarius — MONDAY

10 — TUESDAY

11 — WEDNESDAY

12 ♊ Gemini full moon ○ — THURSDAY

13 — FRIDAY

14 — SATURDAY

15 — SUNDAY

The AstroTwins' 2019 Planetary Planner — 154 —

December 2019

16   MONDAY

17   TUESDAY

18   Waning quarter moon in Virgo ◑   WEDNESDAY

19   THURSDAY

20   ♀ Venus enters Aquarius   FRIDAY

21   ♑ Sun enters Capricorn   SATURDAY

22   SUNDAY

The AstroTwins' 2019 Planetary Planner

December 2019

| 23 | MONDAY |

| 24 | TUESDAY |

| 25 | WEDNESDAY |

| 26 ♑ Capricorn new moon (annular solar eclipse) ● | THURSDAY |

| 27 | FRIDAY |

| 28 ☿ Mercury enters Capricorn | SATURDAY |

| 29 | SUNDAY |

December 2019

30   MONDAY

31   TUESDAY

WEDNESDAY

THURSDAY

FRIDAY

SATURDAY

SUNDAY

OPHIRA & TALI EDUT

Dubbed the "astrologers to the stars," identical twin sisters Ophira and Tali Edut, known as the AstroTwins, are professional astrologers who reach millions worldwide through their spot-on predictions. Through their website, Astrostyle.com, Ophira and Tali help "bring the stars down to earth" with their unique, lifestyle-based approach to astrology.

They are the official astrologers for *ELLE* Magazine and MindBodyGreen.com. The AstroTwins have been featured by major media such as the *Good Morning America*, the *New York Times* and *People* and they've collaborated with major brands including Coach, Vogue, Nordstrom, Revlon, H&M, Urban Outfitters, Ted Baker and 1Hotels.

The sisters have read charts for celebrities including Beyoncé, Stevie Wonder, Emma Roberts, Karlie Kloss and Sting. They have appeared on Bravo's *The Real Housewives of New Jersey*, doing on-air readings for the cast. They have authored numerous print books, including *Love Zodiac, Shoestrology* and *Momstrology* (their #1 Amazon best-selling astrological parenting guide) and a series of self-published books, including their popular annual horoscope guides. ✴

VISIT THE ASTROTWINS AT WWW.ASTROSTYLE.COM
Follow us on social media @astrotwins